THE GUARDIANS OF THE GALAXY ARE CURRENTLY BETWEEN UNIVERSE-ENDING EVENTS THAT NEED STOPPING, SO WE'VE TAKEN A JOB THAT'S CERTAIN TO GET US PAID. IT'S A GOOD THING TO
BEEN BICKERING FOR DAYS AND GAMORA SEE
PUNCH SOMETHING... AND GROOT? WE

ANYWAY... WE'VE GOT A BIG SCORE LINED UP
THIS TIME... WE'RE COLLECTING ON A BOUN
CAPTAIN'S LOG, PREPPING FOR A MISSION A
ABOUT HOW GREAT IT IS TO BE THE LEADER
GROUP OF OUTLAWS THIS SIDE OF

GUARDIANS OF THE GALAXY

THE TELLTALE SERIES

FRED VAN LENTE
WRITER

SALVA ESPIN
ARTIST

JIM CAMPBELL
COLOR ARTIST

VC's CORY PETIT
LETTERER

DAVID NAKAYAMA
COVER ARTIST

DARREN SHAN & CHARLES BEACHAM
EDITORS

JORDAN WHITE
SUPERVISING EDITOR

SPECIAL THANKS

FOR TELLTALE GAMES: JUSTIN LAMBROS, SEAN AINSWORTH, ZACK KELLER AND THE TELLTALE GAMES CREW.

FOR MARVEL GAMES: BILL ROSEMANN, TIM HERNANDEZ, ISABEL HSU AND THE MARVEL GAMES TEAM.

COLLECTION EDITOR MARK D. BEAZLEY ■ ASSISTANT EDITOR CAITLIN O'CONNELL
ASSOCIATE MANAGING EDITOR KATERI WOODY ■ SENIOR EDITOR, SPECIAL PROJECTS JENNIFER GRUNWALD
VP PRODUCTION & SPECIAL PROJECTS JEFF YOUNGQUIST
SVP PRINT, SALES & MARKETING DAVID GABRIEL ■ BOOK DESIGNER JAY BOWEN

EDITOR IN CHIEF C.B. CEBULSKI ■ CHIEF CREATIVE OFFICER JOE QUESADA
PRESIDENT DAN BUCKLEY ■ EXECUTIVE PRODUCER ALAN FINE

GUARDIANS OF THE GALAXY: TELLTALE GAMES. Contains material originally published in magazine form as GUARDIANS OF THE GALAXY TELLTALE GAMES #1-5. First printing 2018. ISBN 978-1-302-90939-0. Published by MARVEL WORLDWIDE, INC., a subsidiary of MARVEL ENTERTAINMENT, LLC. OFFICE OF PUBLICATION: 135 West 50th Street, New York, NY 10020. **Printed in Canada.** DAN BUCKLEY, President, Marvel Entertainment; JOE QUESADA, Chief Creative Officer; TOM BREVOORT, SVP of Publishing; DAVID BOGART, SVP of Business Affairs & Operations, Publishing & Partnership; DAVID GABRIEL, SVP of Sales & Marketing, Publishing; JEFF YOUNGQUIST, VP of Production & Special Projects; DAN CARR, Executive Director of Publishing Technology; ALEX MORALES, Director of Publishing Operations; SUSAN CRESPI, Production Manager; STAN LEE, Chairman Emeritus. For information regarding advertising in Marvel Comics or on Marvel.com, please contact Jonathan Parkhideh, VP of Digital Media & Marketing Solutions, at jparkhideh@marvel.com. For Marvel subscription inquiries, please call 888-511-5480. **Manufactured between 12/1/2017 and 1/2/2018 by SOLISCO PRINTERS, SCOTT, QC, CANADA.**

10 9 8 7 6 5 4 3 2 1

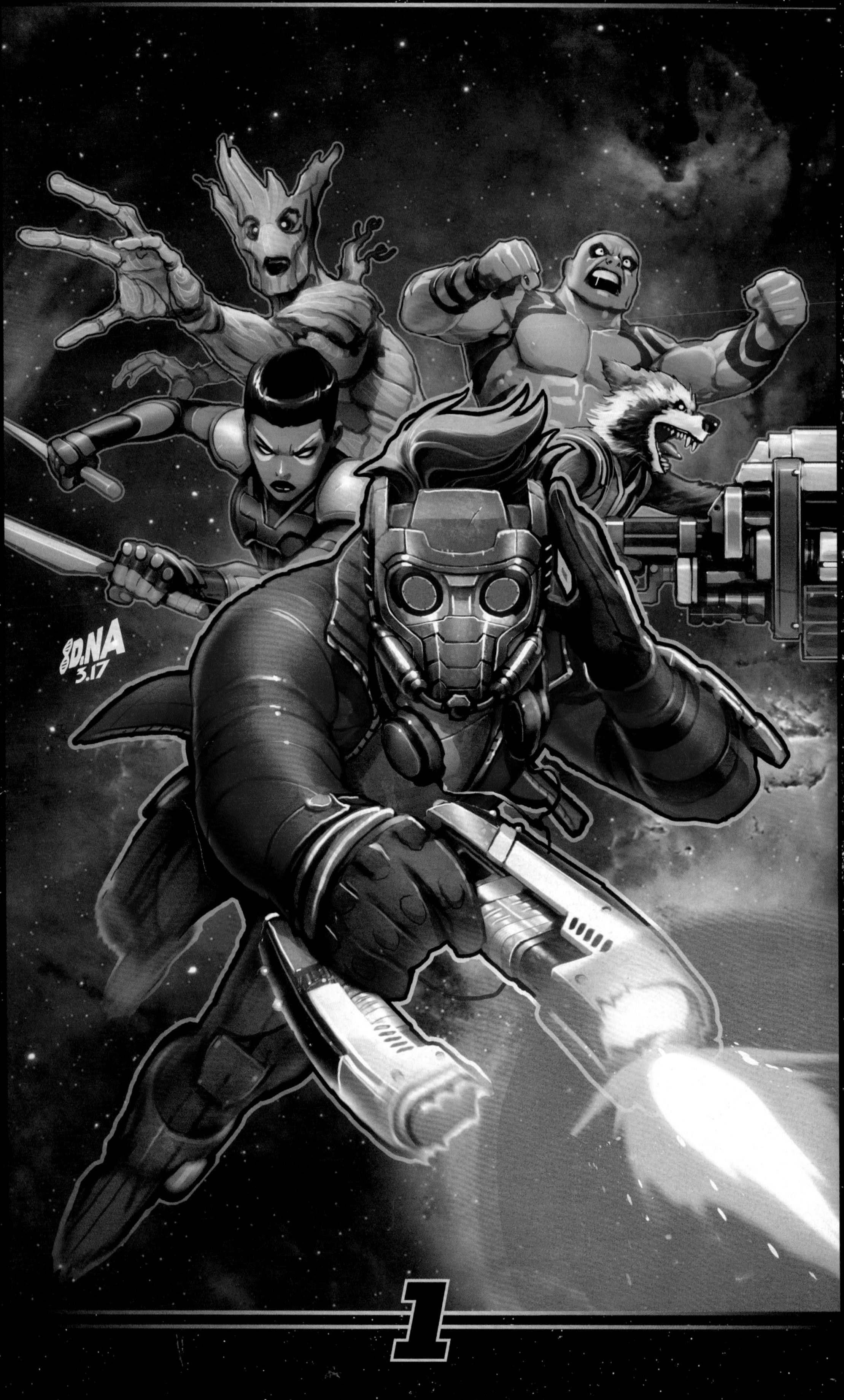
D.NA
3.17
1

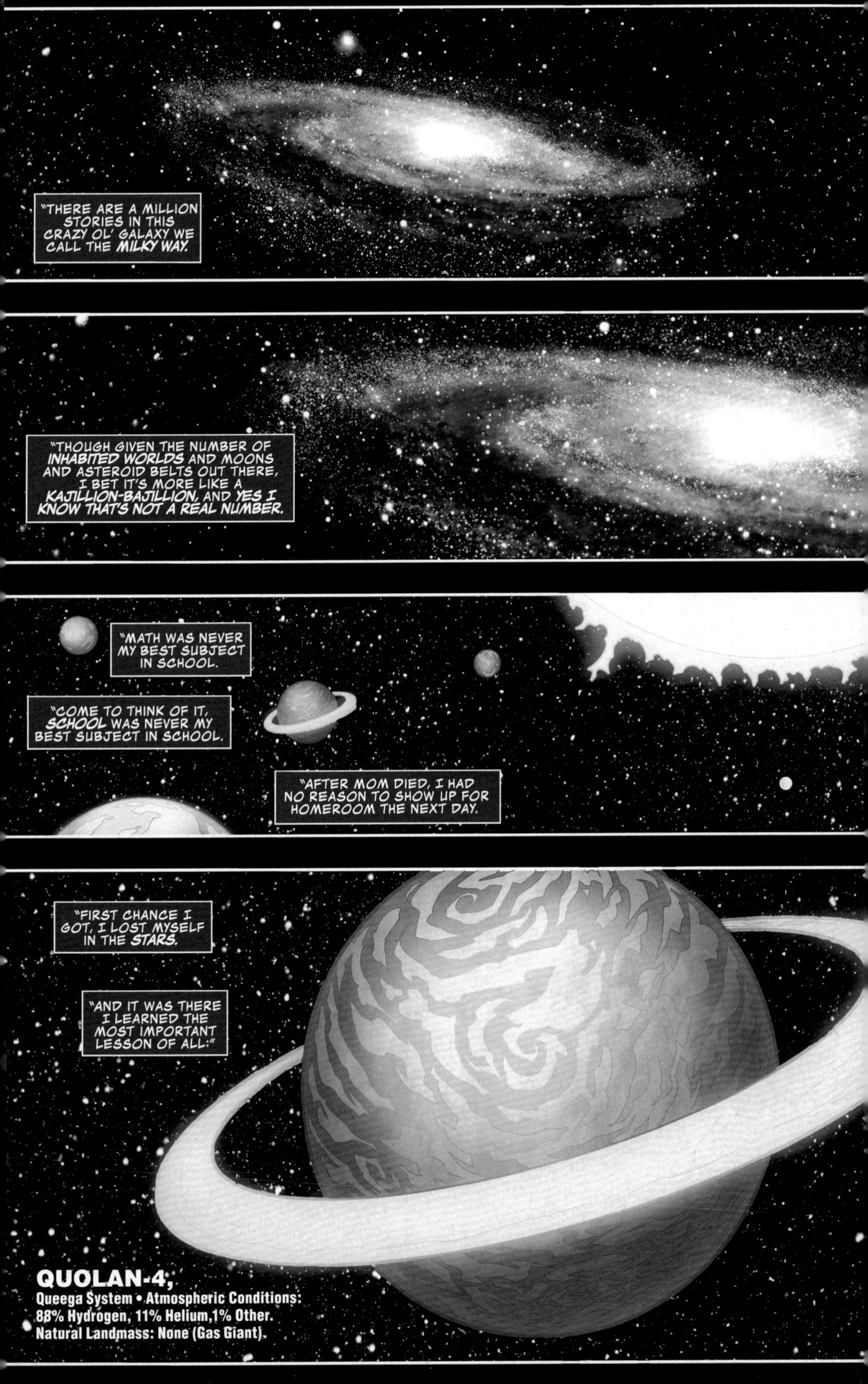
"THERE ARE A MILLION STORIES IN THIS CRAZY OL' GALAXY WE CALL THE MILKY WAY.
"THOUGH GIVEN THE NUMBER OF INHABITED WORLDS AND MOONS AND ASTEROID BELTS OUT THERE, I BET IT'S MORE LIKE A KAJILLION-BAJILLION, AND YES I KNOW THAT'S NOT A REAL NUMBER.
"MATH WAS NEVER MY BEST SUBJECT IN SCHOOL.
"COME TO THINK OF IT, SCHOOL WAS NEVER MY BEST SUBJECT IN SCHOOL.
"AFTER MOM DIED, I HAD NO REASON TO SHOW UP FOR HOMEROOM THE NEXT DAY.
"FIRST CHANCE I GOT, I LOST MYSELF IN THE STARS.
"AND IT WAS THERE I LEARNED THE MOST IMPORTANT LESSON OF ALL:"
QUOLAN-4,
Queega System • Atmospheric Conditions: 88% Hydrogen, 11% Helium,1% Other. Natural Landmass: None (Gas Giant).

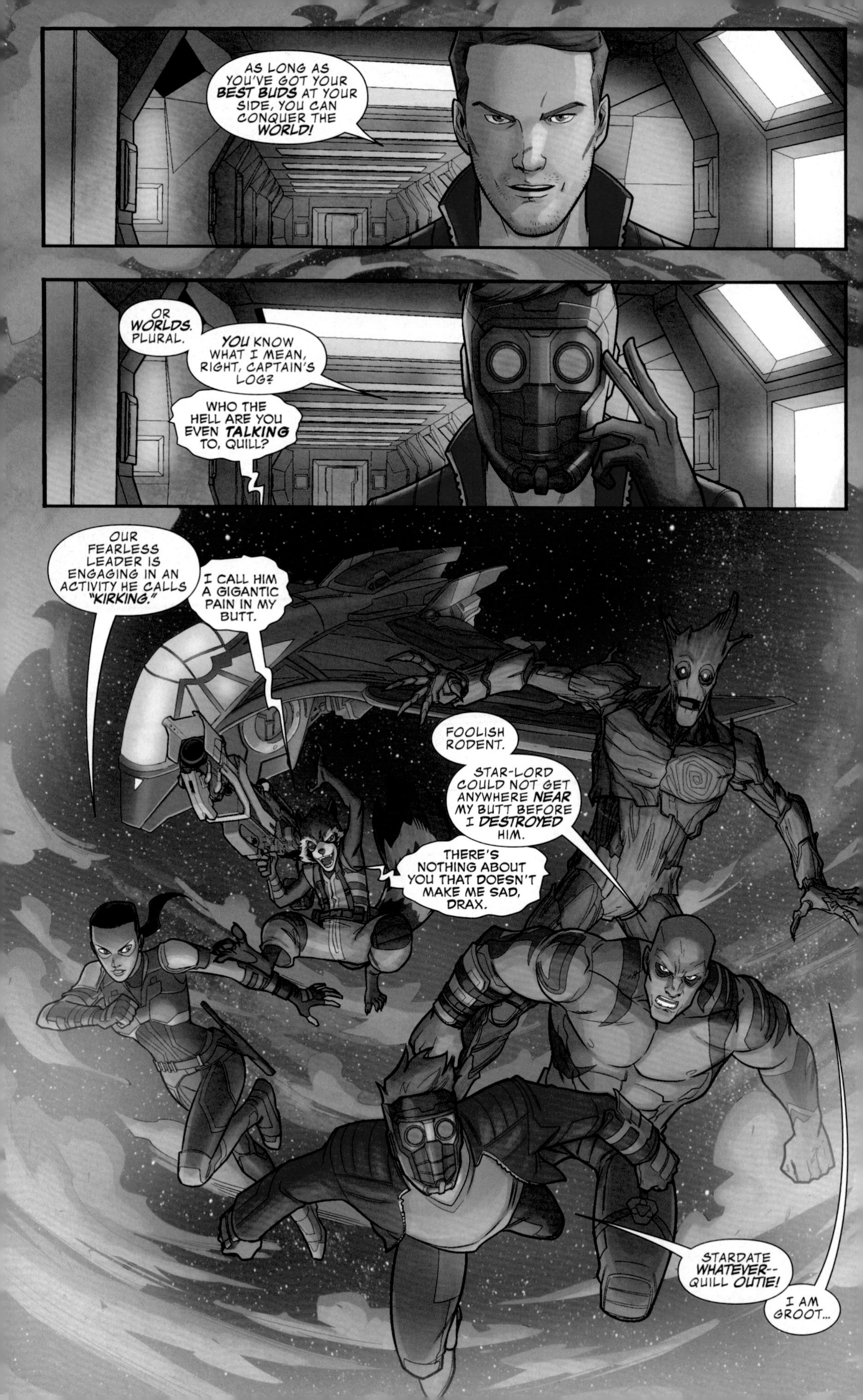
AS LONG AS YOU'VE GOT YOUR BEST BUDS AT YOUR SIDE, YOU CAN CONQUER THE WORLD!
OR WORLDS. PLURAL.
YOU KNOW WHAT I MEAN, RIGHT, CAPTAIN'S LOG?
WHO THE HELL ARE YOU EVEN TALKING TO, QUILL?
OUR FEARLESS LEADER IS ENGAGING IN AN ACTIVITY HE CALLS "KIRKING."
I CALL HIM A GIGANTIC PAIN IN MY BUTT.
FOOLISH RODENT.
STAR-LORD COULD NOT GET ANYWHERE NEAR MY BUTT BEFORE I DESTROYED HIM.
THERE'S NOTHING ABOUT YOU THAT DOESN'T MAKE ME SAD, DRAX.
STARDATE WHATEVER-- QUILL OUTIE!
I AM GROOT...

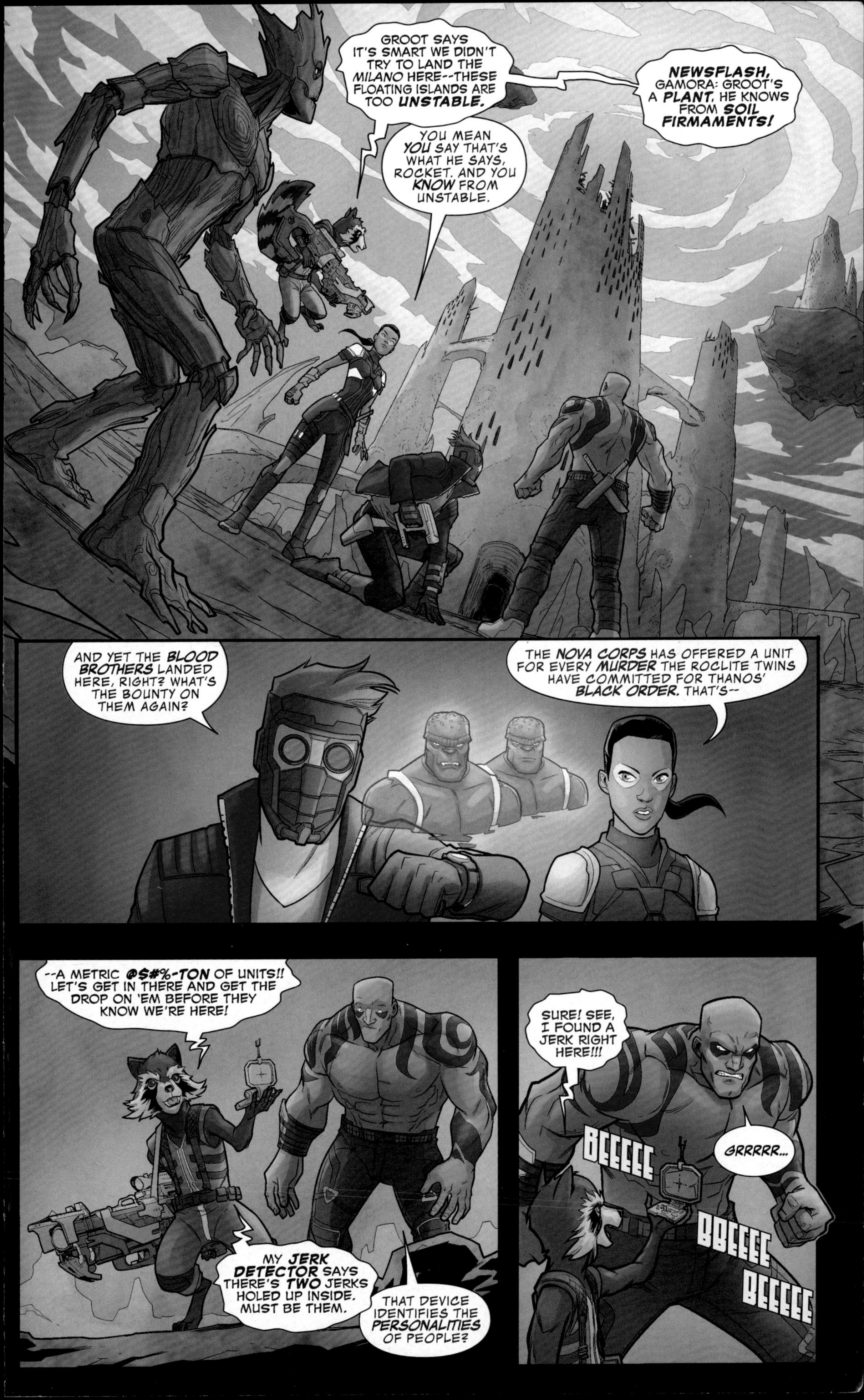
GROOT SAYS IT'S SMART WE DIDN'T TRY TO LAND THE MILANO HERE--THESE FLOATING ISLANDS ARE TOO UNSTABLE.
NEWSFLASH, GAMORA: GROOT'S A PLANT, HE KNOWS FROM SOIL FIRMAMENTS!
YOU MEAN YOU SAY THAT'S WHAT HE SAYS, ROCKET. AND YOU KNOW FROM UNSTABLE.
AND YET THE BLOOD BROTHERS LANDED HERE, RIGHT? WHAT'S THE BOUNTY ON THEM AGAIN?
THE NOVA CORPS HAS OFFERED A UNIT FOR EVERY MURDER THE ROCLITE TWINS HAVE COMMITTED FOR THANOS' BLACK ORDER. THAT'S--
--A METRIC @$#%-TON OF UNITS!! LET'S GET IN THERE AND GET THE DROP ON 'EM BEFORE THEY KNOW WE'RE HERE!
MY JERK DETECTOR SAYS THERE'S TWO JERKS HOLED UP INSIDE. MUST BE THEM.
THAT DEVICE IDENTIFIES THE PERSONALITIES OF PEOPLE?
SURE! SEE, I FOUND A JERK RIGHT HERE!!!
BEEEEE
GRRRRR...
BBEEEE
BEEEEE

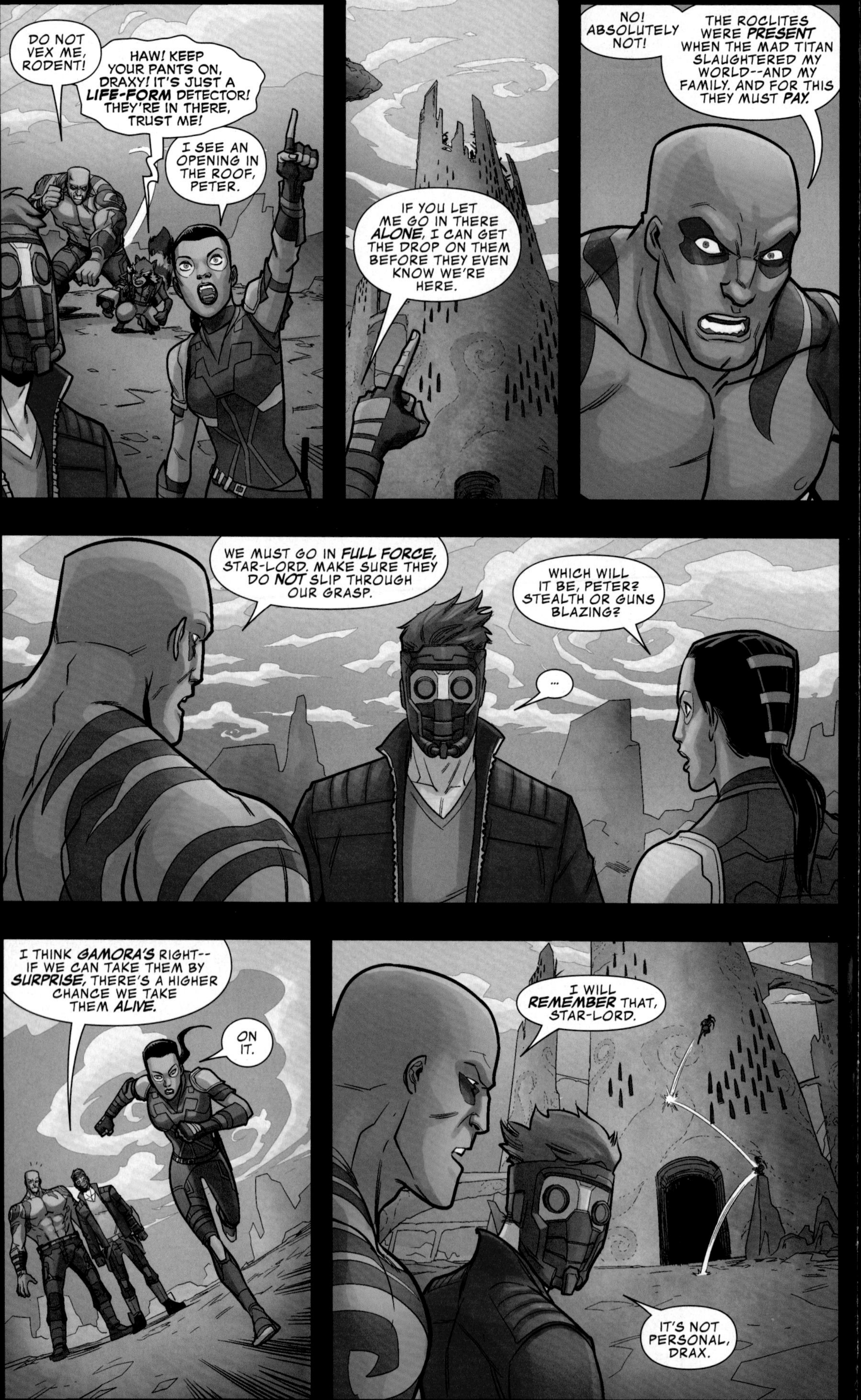
DO NOT VEX ME, RODENT!
HAW! KEEP YOUR PANTS ON, DRAXY! IT'S JUST A LIFE-FORM DETECTOR! THEY'RE IN THERE, TRUST ME!
I SEE AN OPENING IN THE ROOF, PETER.
IF YOU LET ME GO IN THERE ALONE, I CAN GET THE DROP ON THEM BEFORE THEY EVEN KNOW WE'RE HERE.
NO! ABSOLUTELY NOT!
THE ROCLITES WERE PRESENT WHEN THE MAD TITAN SLAUGHTERED MY WORLD--AND MY FAMILY. AND FOR THIS THEY MUST PAY.
WE MUST GO IN FULL FORCE, STAR-LORD. MAKE SURE THEY DO NOT SLIP THROUGH OUR GRASP.
WHICH WILL IT BE, PETER? STEALTH OR GUNS BLAZING?
...
I THINK GAMORA'S RIGHT-- IF WE CAN TAKE THEM BY SURPRISE, THERE'S A HIGHER CHANCE WE TAKE THEM ALIVE.
ON IT.
I WILL REMEMBER THAT, STAR-LORD.
IT'S NOT PERSONAL, DRAX.

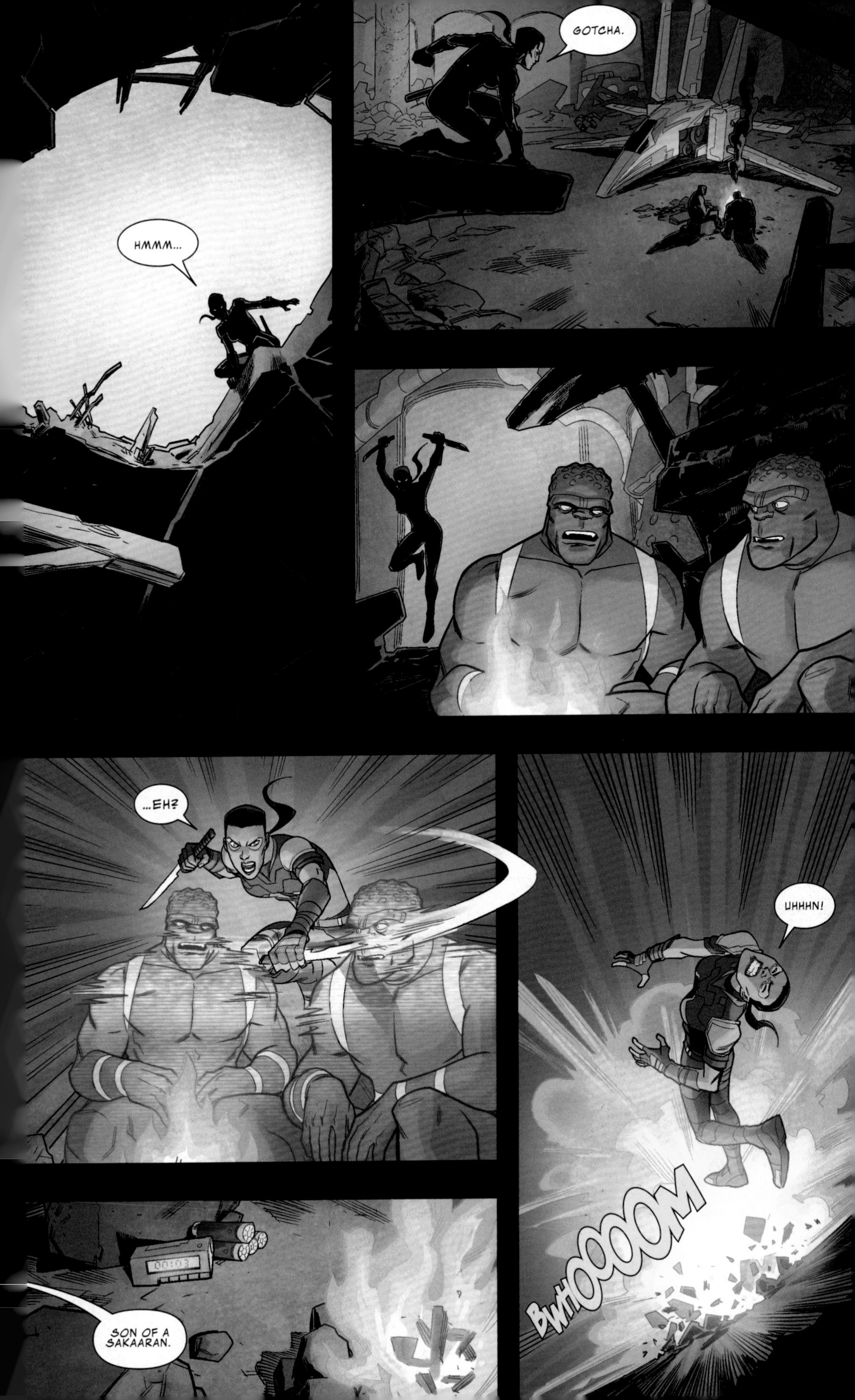
HMMM...
GOTCHA.
...EH?
UHHHN!
SON OF A SAKAARAN.
00:03
BWHOOOOM

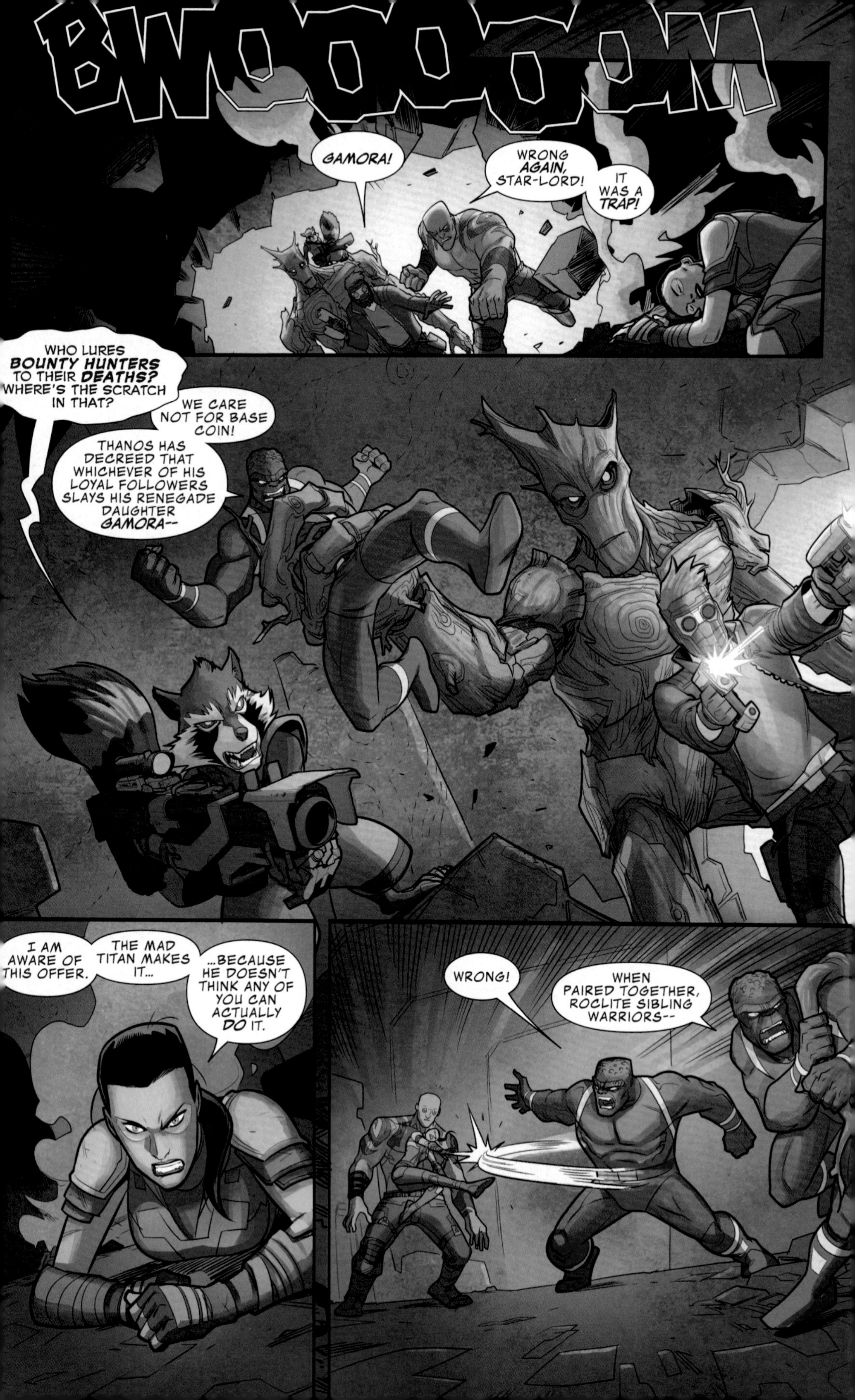
BWOOOOOM
GAMORA!
WRONG AGAIN, STAR-LORD!
IT WAS A TRAP!
WHO LURES BOUNTY HUNTERS TO THEIR DEATHS? WHERE'S THE SCRATCH IN THAT?
WE CARE NOT FOR BASE COIN!
THANOS HAS DECREED THAT WHICHEVER OF HIS LOYAL FOLLOWERS SLAYS HIS RENEGADE DAUGHTER GAMORA--
I AM AWARE OF THIS OFFER.
THE MAD TITAN MAKES IT...
...BECAUSE HE DOESN'T THINK ANY OF YOU CAN ACTUALLY DO IT.
WRONG!
WHEN PAIRED TOGETHER, ROCLITE SIBLING WARRIORS--

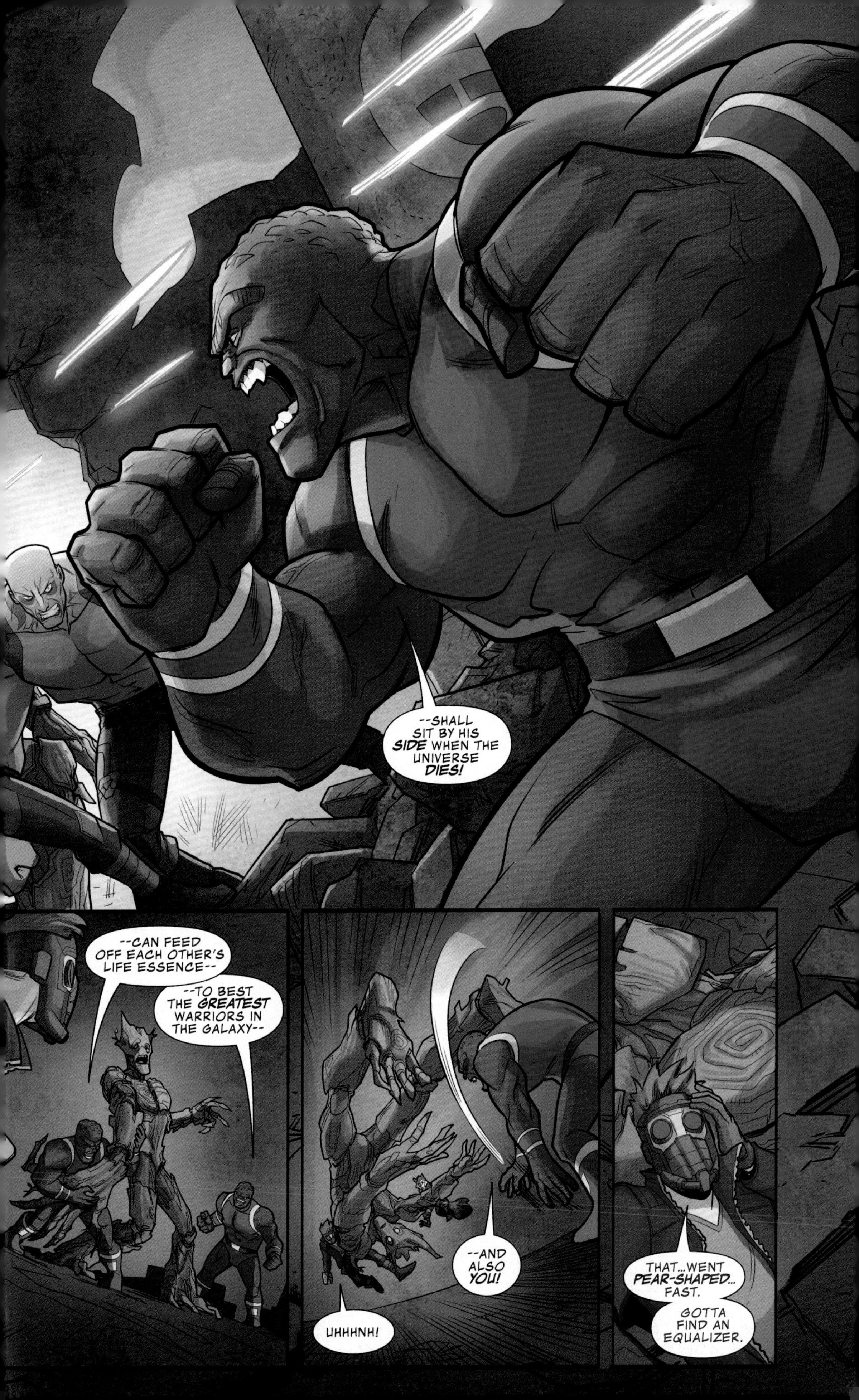
--SHALL SIT BY HIS SIDE WHEN THE UNIVERSE DIES!
--CAN FEED OFF EACH OTHER'S LIFE ESSENCE--
--TO BEST THE GREATEST WARRIORS IN THE GALAXY--
--AND ALSO YOU!
UHHHNH!
THAT...WENT PEAR-SHAPED... FAST.
GOTTA FIND AN EQUALIZER.

LOOK AT:

ANCIENT ALIEN, UH, THINGIES

LOOK AT:

ROCKET'S BFG

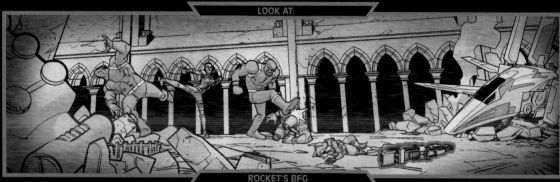

LOOK AT:

STOLEN NOVA CORPS SHIP

HMMM....

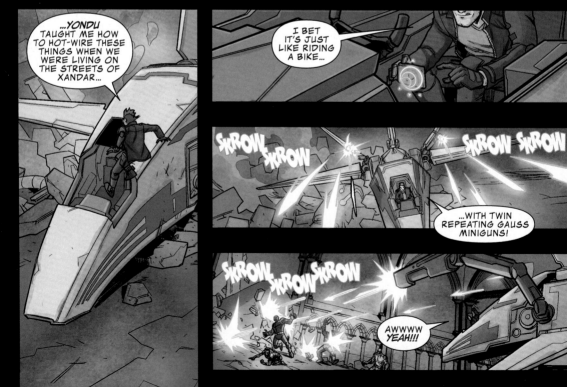

...YONDU TAUGHT ME HOW TO HOT-WIRE THESE THINGS WHEN WE WERE LIVING ON THE STREETS OF XANDAR...

I BET IT'S JUST LIKE RIDING A BIKE...

SKROW SKROW

SKROW SKROW

...WITH TWIN REPEATING GAUSS MINIGUNS!

SKROW SKROW SKROW

AWWWW YEAH!!!

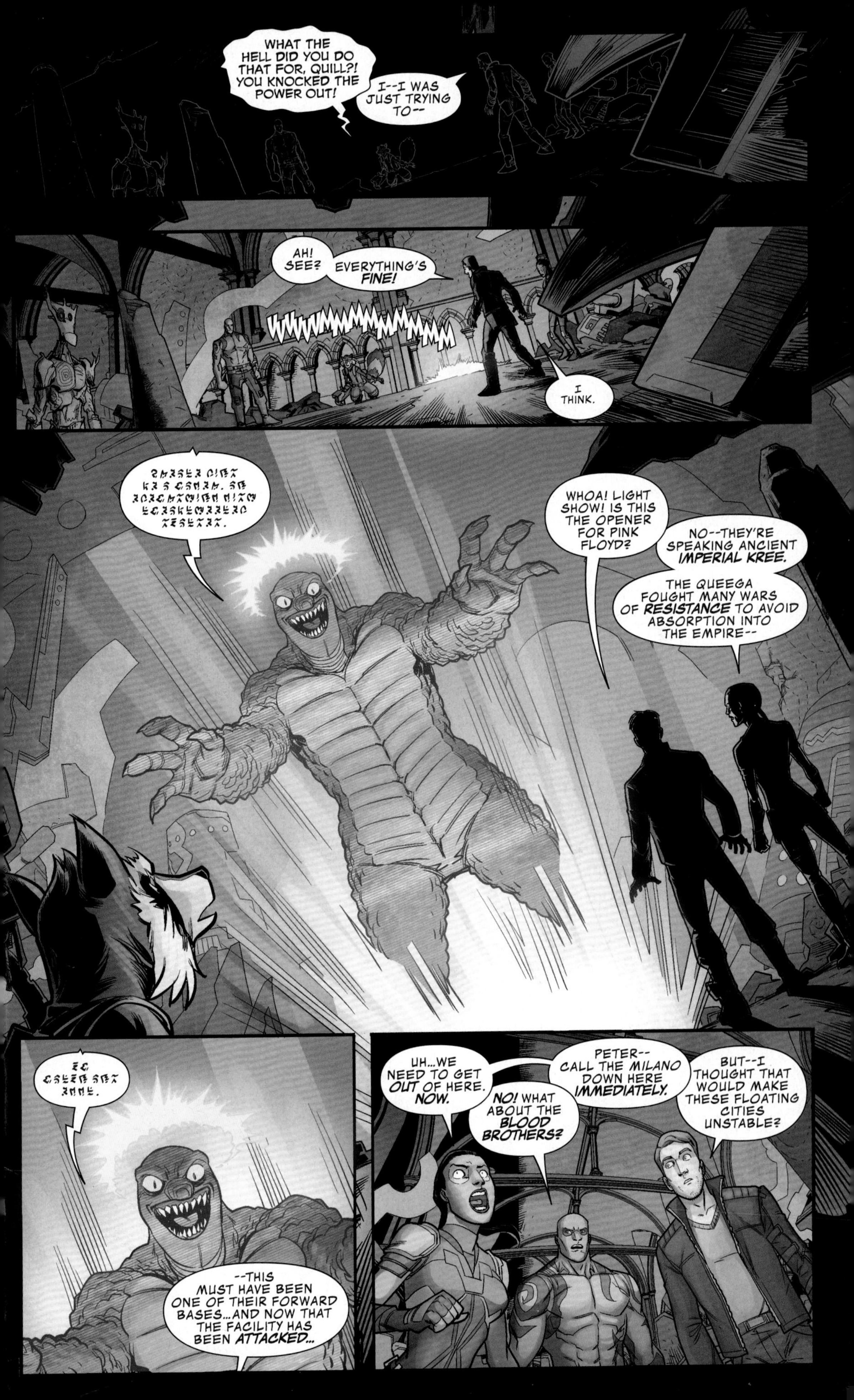
WHAT THE HELL DID YOU DO THAT FOR, QUILL?! YOU KNOCKED THE POWER OUT!
I--I WAS JUST TRYING TO--
AH! SEE?
EVERYTHING'S FINE!
WHUMMMMMMMMMMMMM
I THINK.
WHOA! LIGHT SHOW! IS THIS THE OPENER FOR PINK FLOYD?
NO--THEY'RE SPEAKING ANCIENT IMPERIAL KREE.
THE QUEEGA FOUGHT MANY WARS OF RESISTANCE TO AVOID ABSORPTION INTO THE EMPIRE--
--THIS MUST HAVE BEEN ONE OF THEIR FORWARD BASES...AND NOW THAT THE FACILITY HAS BEEN ATTACKED...
UH...WE NEED TO GET OUT OF HERE. NOW.
PETER--CALL THE MILANO DOWN HERE IMMEDIATELY.
NO! WHAT ABOUT THE BLOOD BROTHERS?
BUT--I THOUGHT THAT WOULD MAKE THESE FLOATING CITIES UNSTABLE?

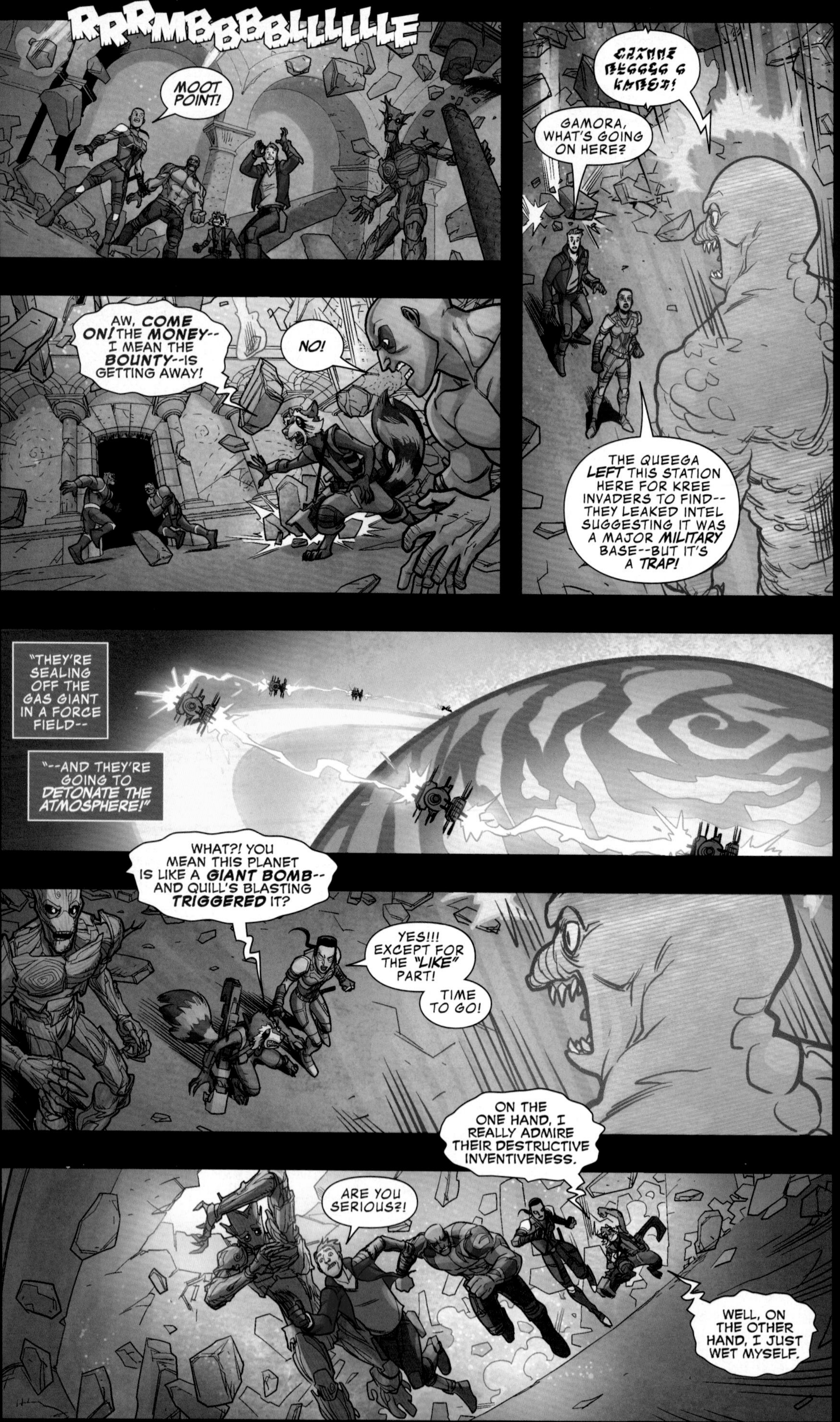
RRRMBBBBLLLLLLE
MOOT POINT!
GAMORA, WHAT'S GOING ON HERE?
AW, COME ON! THE MONEY-- I MEAN THE BOUNTY--IS GETTING AWAY!
NO!
THE QUEEGA LEFT THIS STATION HERE FOR KREE INVADERS TO FIND-- THEY LEAKED INTEL SUGGESTING IT WAS A MAJOR MILITARY BASE--BUT IT'S A TRAP!
"THEY'RE SEALING OFF THE GAS GIANT IN A FORCE FIELD--
"--AND THEY'RE GOING TO DETONATE THE ATMOSPHERE!"
WHAT?! YOU MEAN THIS PLANET IS LIKE A GIANT BOMB-- AND QUILL'S BLASTING TRIGGERED IT?
YES!!! EXCEPT FOR THE "LIKE" PART!
TIME TO GO!
ON THE ONE HAND, I REALLY ADMIRE THEIR DESTRUCTIVE INVENTIVENESS.
ARE YOU SERIOUS?!
WELL, ON THE OTHER HAND, I JUST WET MYSELF.

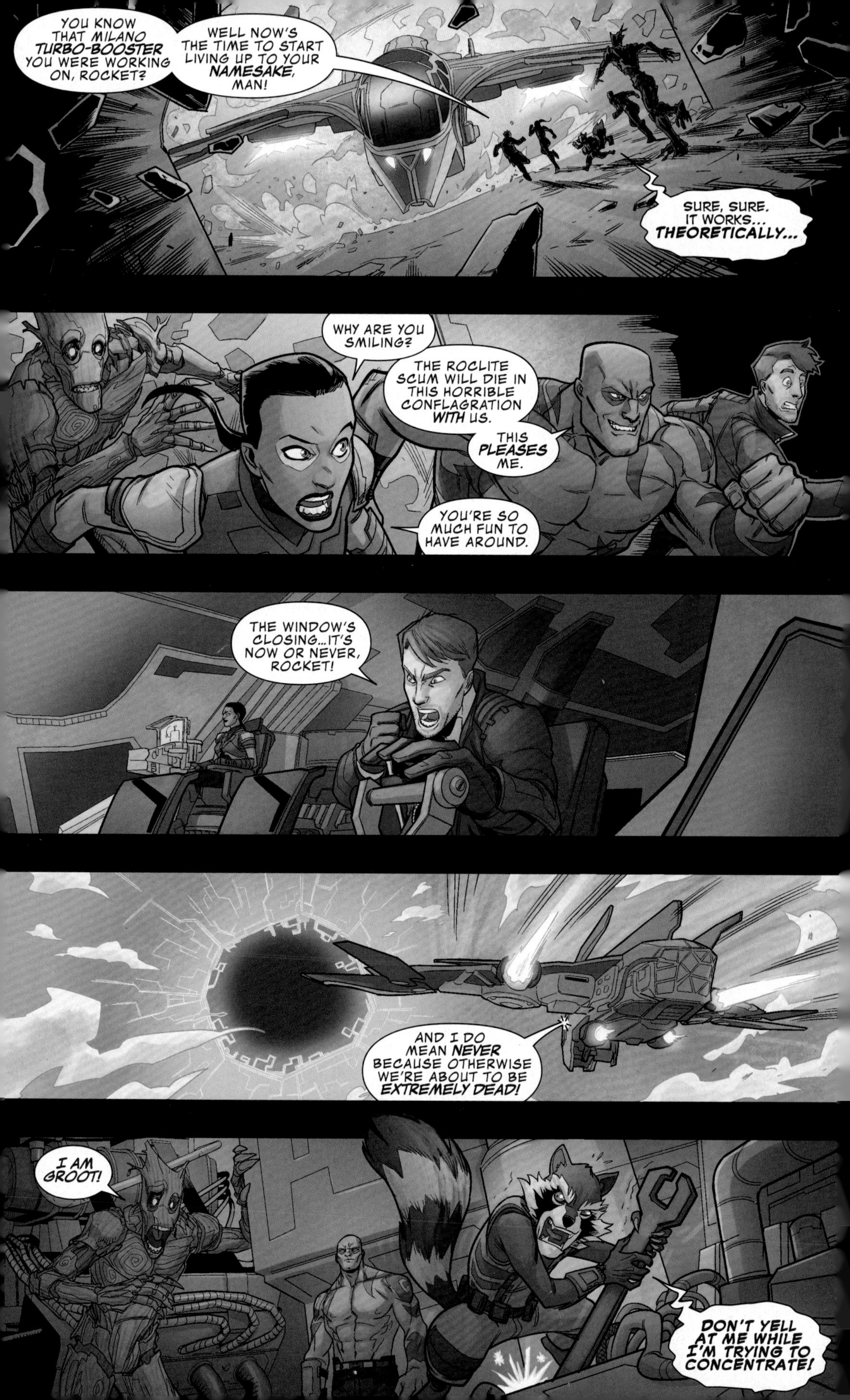
YOU KNOW THAT MILANO TURBO-BOOSTER YOU WERE WORKING ON, ROCKET?
WELL NOW'S THE TIME TO START LIVING UP TO YOUR NAMESAKE, MAN!
SURE, SURE. IT WORKS... THEORETICALLY...
WHY ARE YOU SMILING?
THE ROCLITE SCUM WILL DIE IN THIS HORRIBLE CONFLAGRATION WITH US.
THIS PLEASES ME.
YOU'RE SO MUCH FUN TO HAVE AROUND.
THE WINDOW'S CLOSING...IT'S NOW OR NEVER, ROCKET!
AND I DO MEAN NEVER BECAUSE OTHERWISE WE'RE ABOUT TO BE EXTREMELY DEAD!
I AM GROOT!
DON'T YELL AT ME WHILE I'M TRYING TO CONCENTRATE!

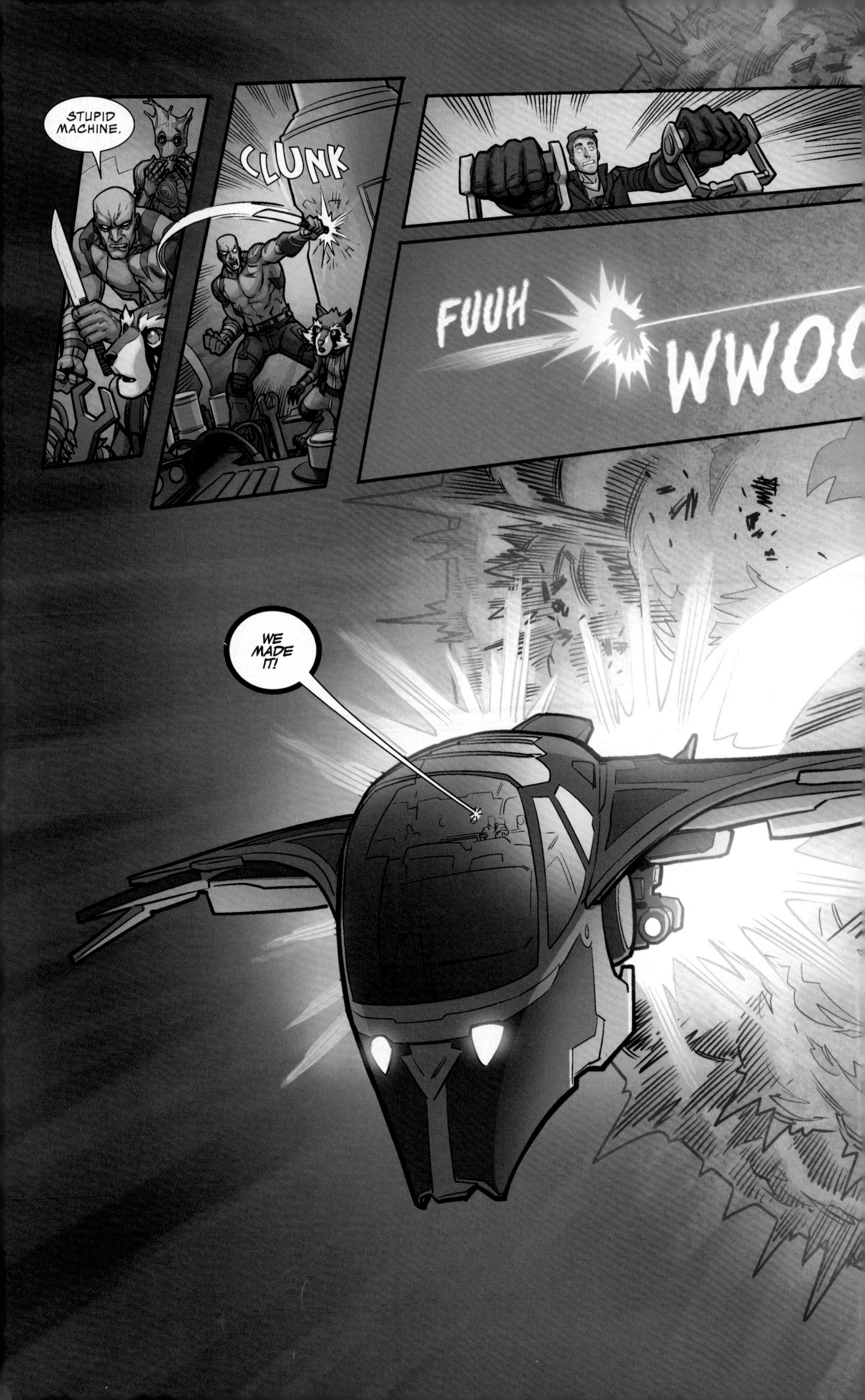
STUPID MACHINE.
CLUNK
FUUH
WWOO
WE MADE IT!

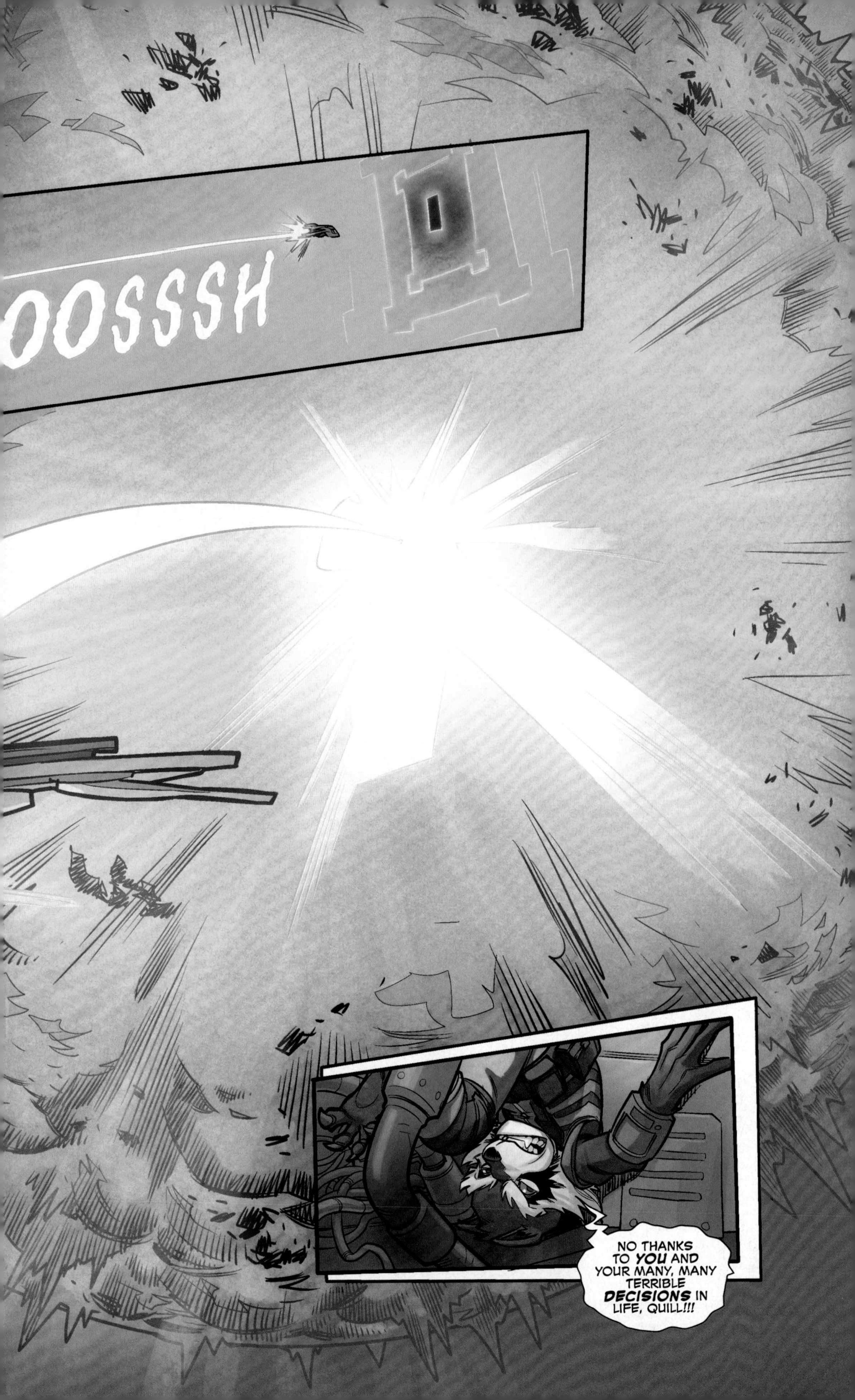
OOSSSH
NO THANKS TO YOU AND YOUR MANY, MANY TERRIBLE DECISIONS IN LIFE, QUILL!!!

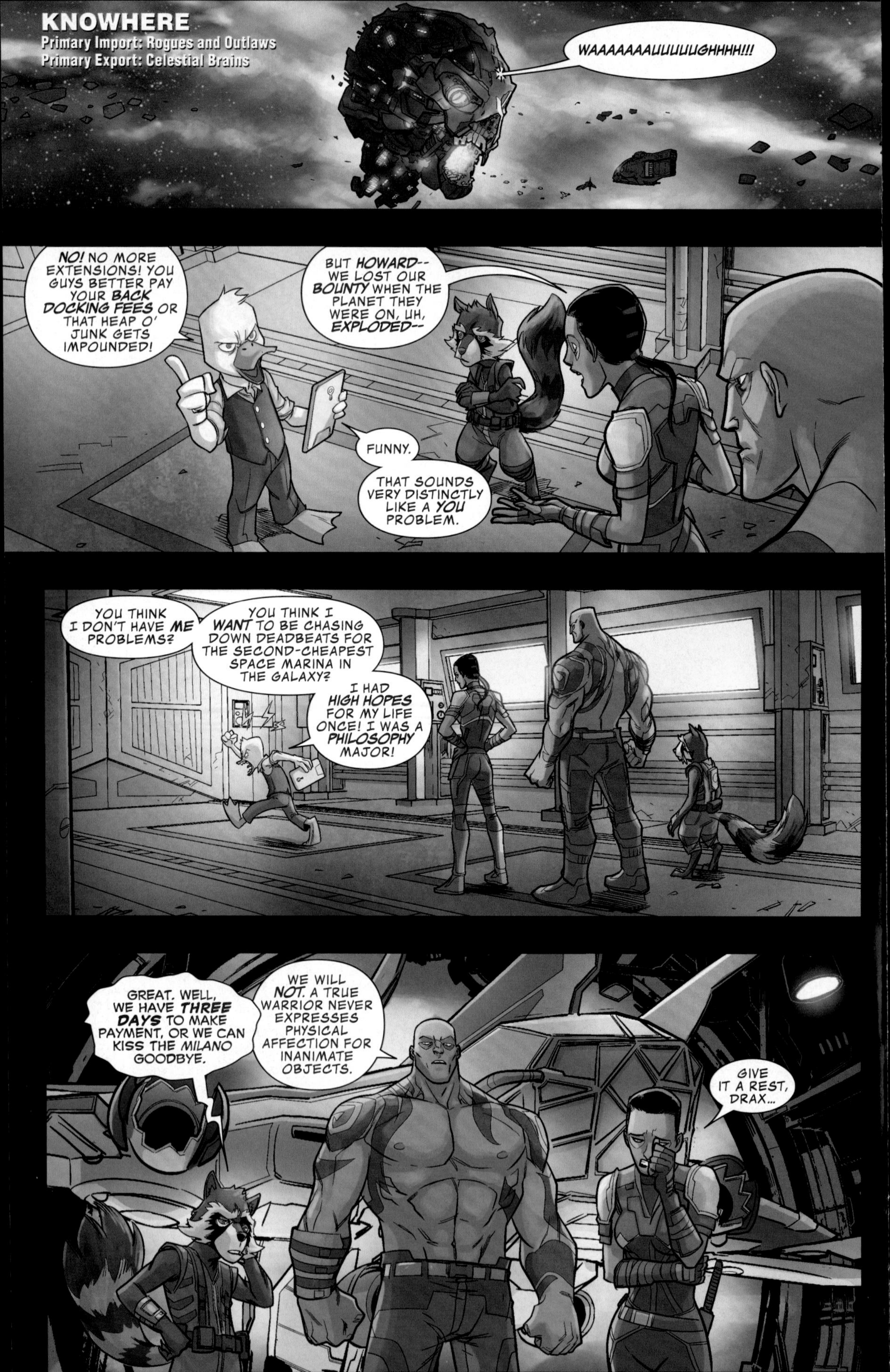
KNOWHERE
Primary Import: Rogues and Outlaws
Primary Export: Celestial Brains
WAAAAAAAUUUUUGHHHH!!!
NO! NO MORE EXTENSIONS! YOU GUYS BETTER PAY YOUR BACK DOCKING FEES OR THAT HEAP O' JUNK GETS IMPOUNDED!
BUT HOWARD-- WE LOST OUR BOUNTY WHEN THE PLANET THEY WERE ON, UH, EXPLODED--
FUNNY.
THAT SOUNDS VERY DISTINCTLY LIKE A YOU PROBLEM.
YOU THINK I DON'T HAVE ME PROBLEMS?
YOU THINK I WANT TO BE CHASING DOWN DEADBEATS FOR THE SECOND-CHEAPEST SPACE MARINA IN THE GALAXY?
I HAD HIGH HOPES FOR MY LIFE ONCE! I WAS A PHILOSOPHY MAJOR!
GREAT. WELL, WE HAVE THREE DAYS TO MAKE PAYMENT, OR WE CAN KISS THE MILANO GOODBYE.
WE WILL NOT. A TRUE WARRIOR NEVER EXPRESSES PHYSICAL AFFECTION FOR INANIMATE OBJECTS.
GIVE IT A REST, DRAX...

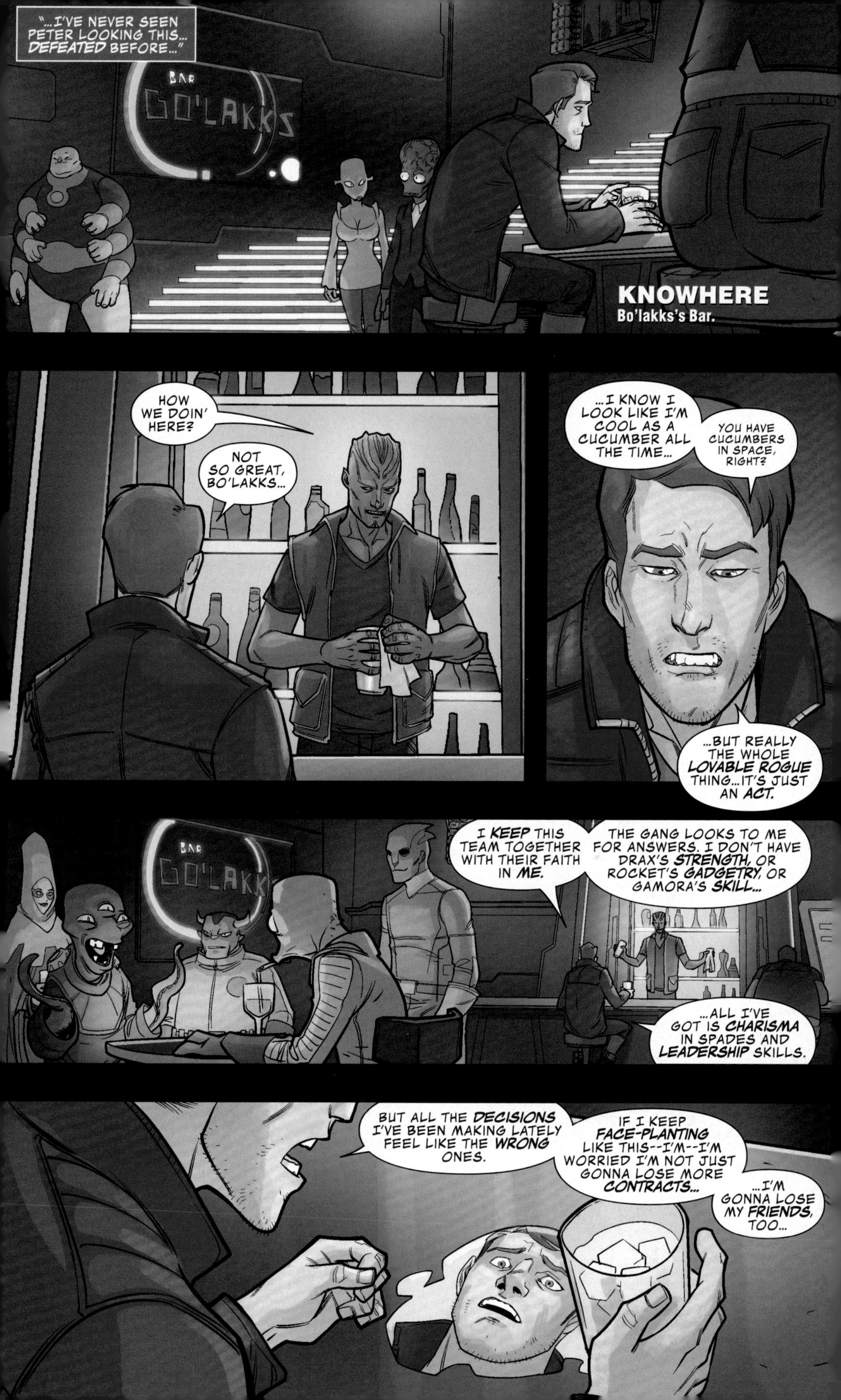
"...I'VE NEVER SEEN PETER LOOKING THIS... DEFEATED BEFORE..."
BAR BO'LAKKS
KNOWHERE
Bo'lakks's Bar.
HOW WE DOIN' HERE?
NOT SO GREAT, BO'LAKKS...
...I KNOW I LOOK LIKE I'M COOL AS A CUCUMBER ALL THE TIME...
YOU HAVE CUCUMBERS IN SPACE, RIGHT?
...BUT REALLY THE WHOLE LOVABLE ROGUE THING...IT'S JUST AN ACT.
BAR BO'LAKKS
I KEEP THIS TEAM TOGETHER WITH THEIR FAITH IN ME.
THE GANG LOOKS TO ME FOR ANSWERS. I DON'T HAVE DRAX'S STRENGTH, OR ROCKET'S GADGETRY, OR GAMORA'S SKILL...
...ALL I'VE GOT IS CHARISMA IN SPADES AND LEADERSHIP SKILLS.
BUT ALL THE DECISIONS I'VE BEEN MAKING LATELY FEEL LIKE THE WRONG ONES.
IF I KEEP FACE-PLANTING LIKE THIS--I'M--I'M WORRIED I'M NOT JUST GONNA LOSE MORE CONTRACTS...
...I'M GONNA LOSE MY FRIENDS, TOO...

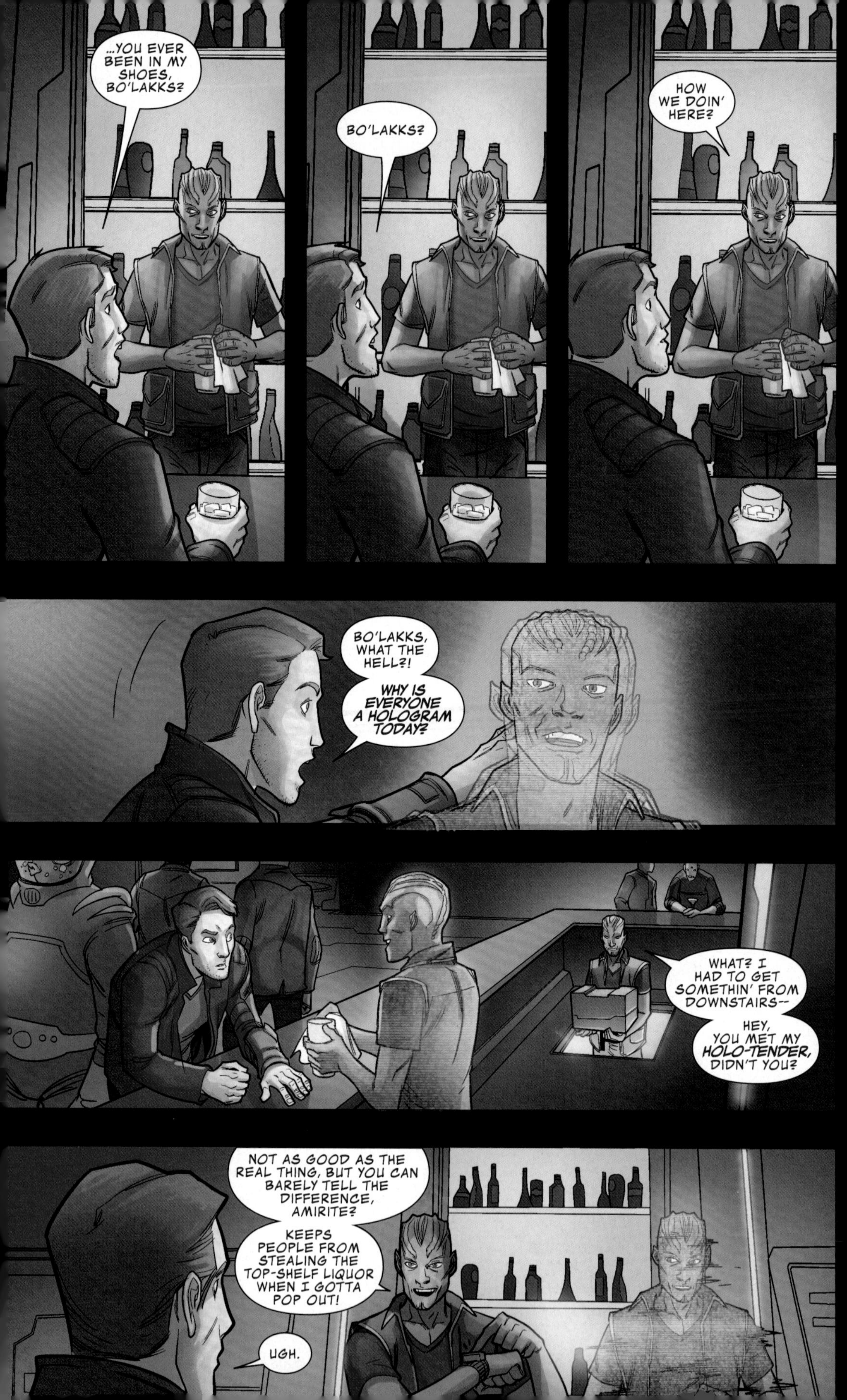

...YOU EVER BEEN IN MY SHOES, BO'LAKKS?
BO'LAKKS?
HOW WE DOIN' HERE?
BO'LAKKS, WHAT THE HELL?!
WHY IS EVERYONE A HOLOGRAM TODAY?
WHAT? I HAD TO GET SOMETHIN' FROM DOWNSTAIRS--
HEY, YOU MET MY HOLO-TENDER, DIDN'T YOU?
NOT AS GOOD AS THE REAL THING, BUT YOU CAN BARELY TELL THE DIFFERENCE, AMIRITE?
KEEPS PEOPLE FROM STEALING THE TOP-SHELF LIQUOR WHEN I GOTTA POP OUT!
UGH.

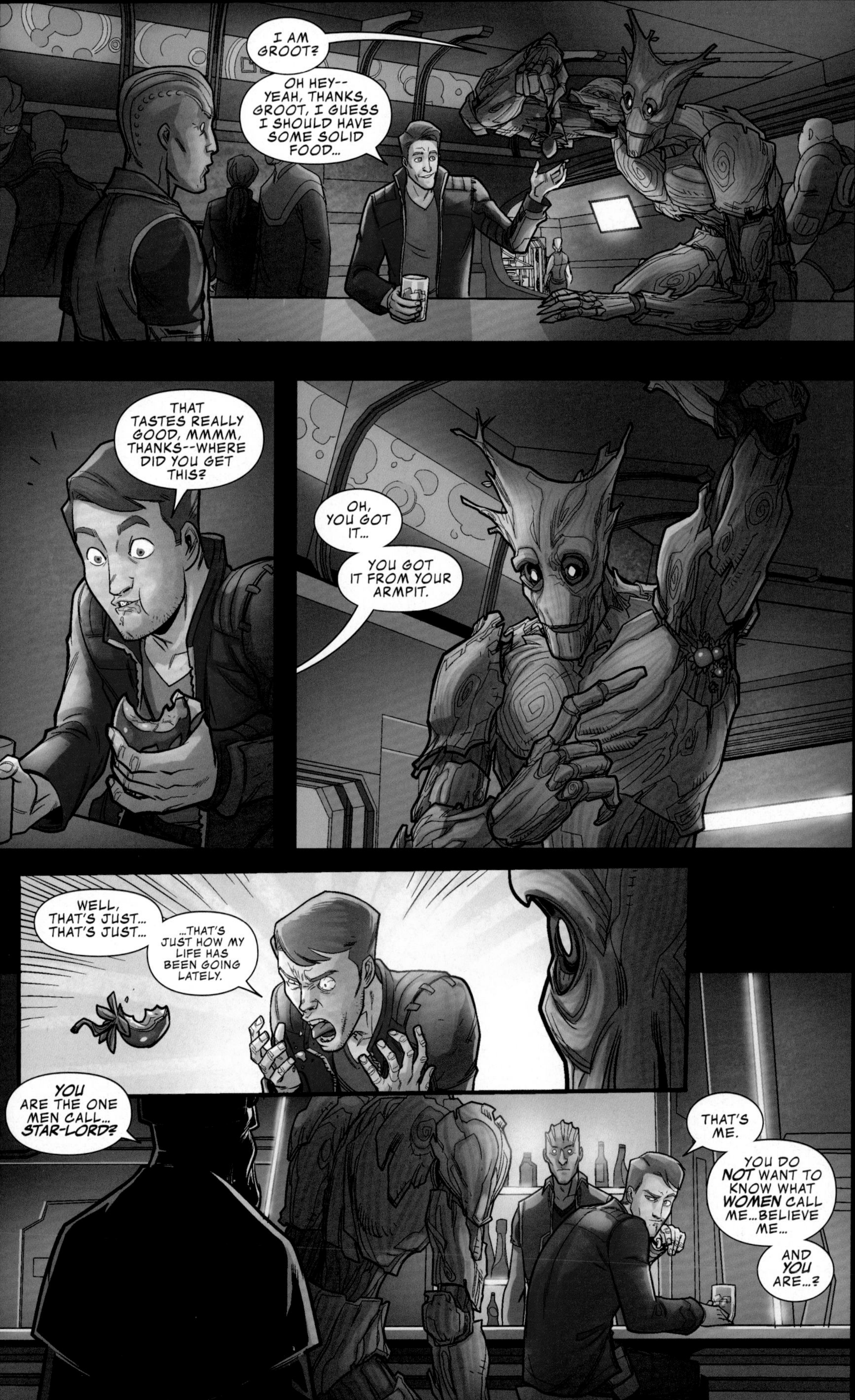
I AM GROOT?
OH HEY-- YEAH, THANKS, GROOT, I GUESS I SHOULD HAVE SOME SOLID FOOD...
THAT TASTES REALLY GOOD, MMMM, THANKS--WHERE DID YOU GET THIS?
OH, YOU GOT IT...
YOU GOT IT FROM YOUR ARMPIT.
WELL, THAT'S JUST... THAT'S JUST...
...THAT'S JUST HOW MY LIFE HAS BEEN GOING LATELY.
YOU ARE THE ONE MEN CALL... STAR-LORD?
THAT'S ME.
YOU DO NOT WANT TO KNOW WHAT WOMEN CALL ME...BELIEVE ME...
AND YOU ARE...?

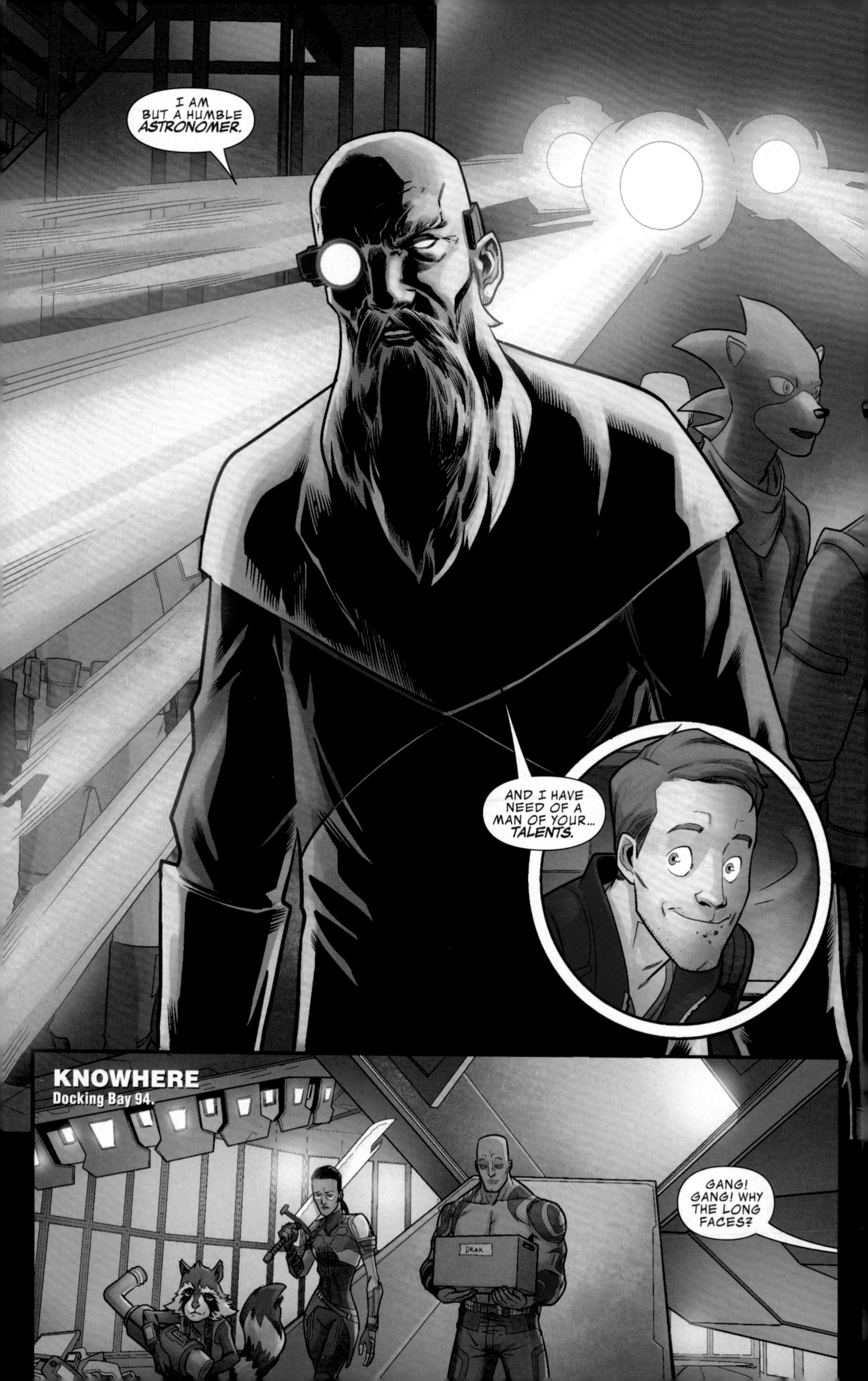
I AM BUT A HUMBLE ASTRONOMER.
AND I HAVE NEED OF A MAN OF YOUR... TALENTS.
KNOWHERE
Docking Bay 94.
GANG! GANG! WHY THE LONG FACES?
DRAX

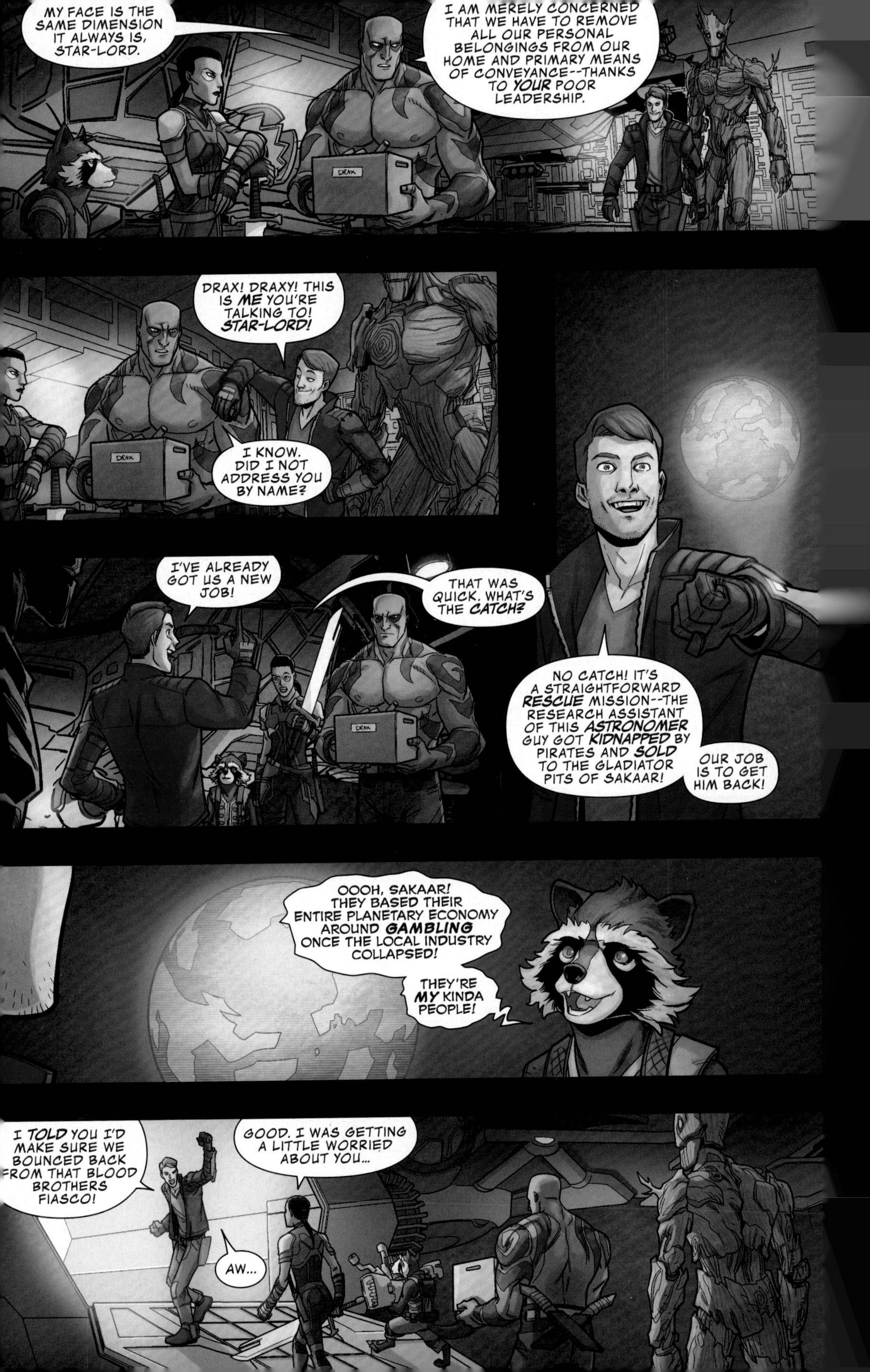

MY FACE IS THE SAME DIMENSION IT ALWAYS IS, STAR-LORD.
I AM MERELY CONCERNED THAT WE HAVE TO REMOVE ALL OUR PERSONAL BELONGINGS FROM OUR HOME AND PRIMARY MEANS OF CONVEYANCE--THANKS TO YOUR POOR LEADERSHIP.
DRAX
DRAX! DRAXY! THIS IS ME YOU'RE TALKING TO! STAR-LORD!
I KNOW. DID I NOT ADDRESS YOU BY NAME?
DRAX
I'VE ALREADY GOT US A NEW JOB!
THAT WAS QUICK. WHAT'S THE CATCH?
DRAX
NO CATCH! IT'S A STRAIGHTFORWARD RESCUE MISSION--THE RESEARCH ASSISTANT OF THIS ASTRONOMER GUY GOT KIDNAPPED BY PIRATES AND SOLD TO THE GLADIATOR PITS OF SAKAAR!
OUR JOB IS TO GET HIM BACK!
OOOH, SAKAAR! THEY BASED THEIR ENTIRE PLANETARY ECONOMY AROUND GAMBLING ONCE THE LOCAL INDUSTRY COLLAPSED!
THEY'RE MY KINDA PEOPLE!
I TOLD YOU I'D MAKE SURE WE BOUNCED BACK FROM THAT BLOOD BROTHERS FIASCO!
GOOD. I WAS GETTING A LITTLE WORRIED ABOUT YOU...
AW...

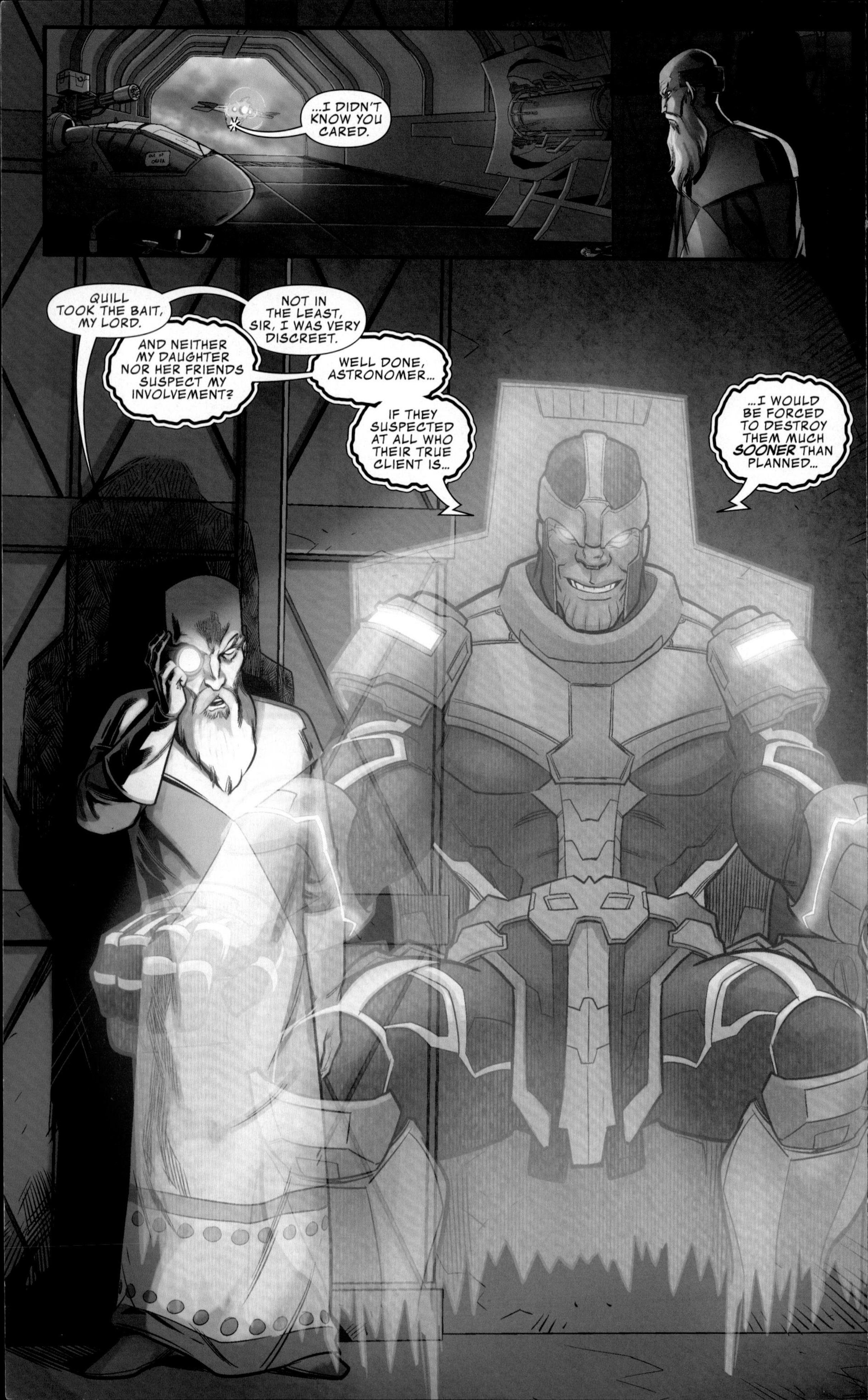
...I DIDN'T KNOW YOU CARED.
QUILL TOOK THE BAIT, MY LORD.
NOT IN THE LEAST, SIR, I WAS VERY DISCREET.
AND NEITHER MY DAUGHTER NOR HER FRIENDS SUSPECT MY INVOLVEMENT?
WELL DONE, ASTRONOMER...
IF THEY SUSPECTED AT ALL WHO THEIR TRUE CLIENT IS...
...I WOULD BE FORCED TO DESTROY THEM MUCH SOONER THAN PLANNED...

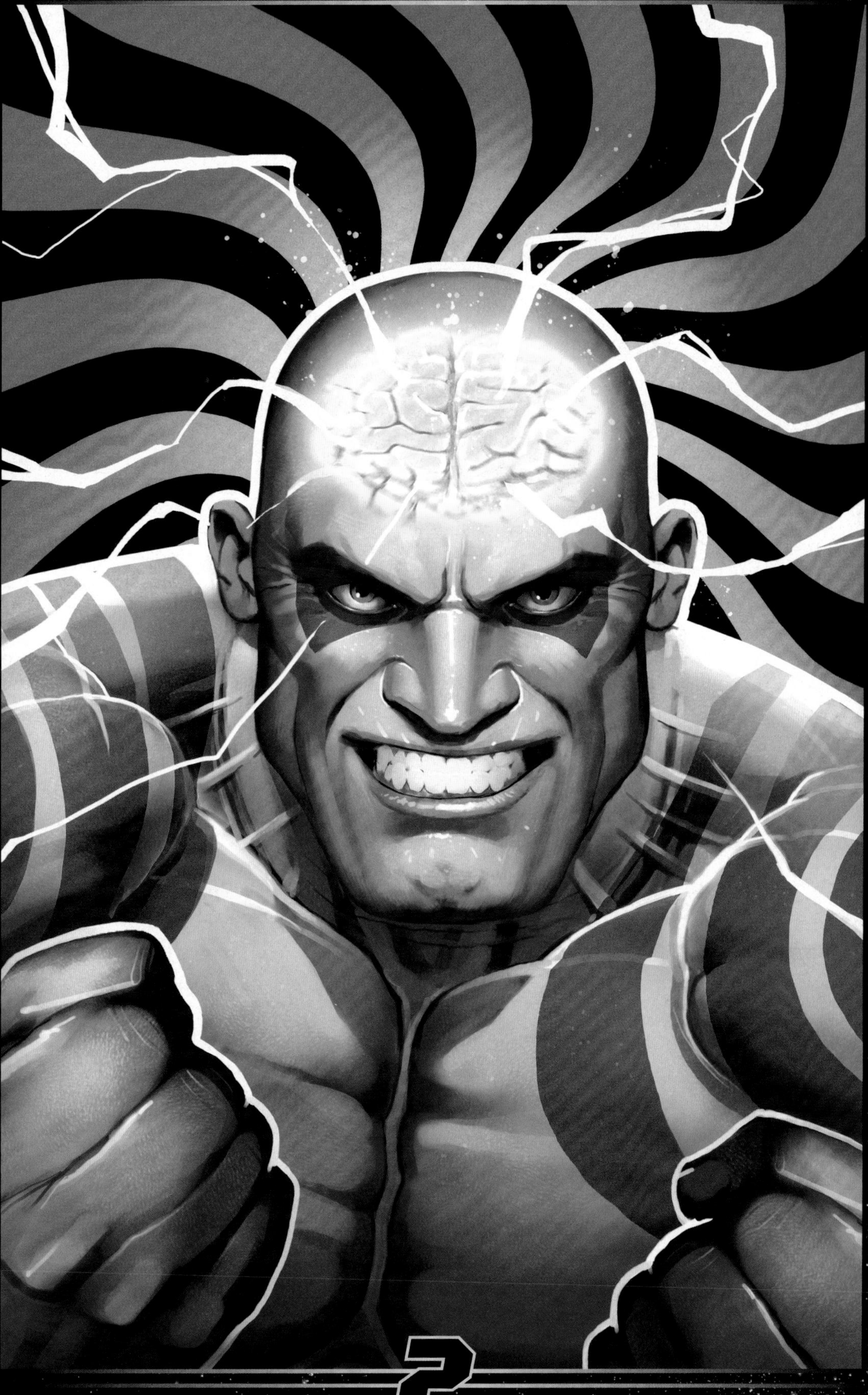
2

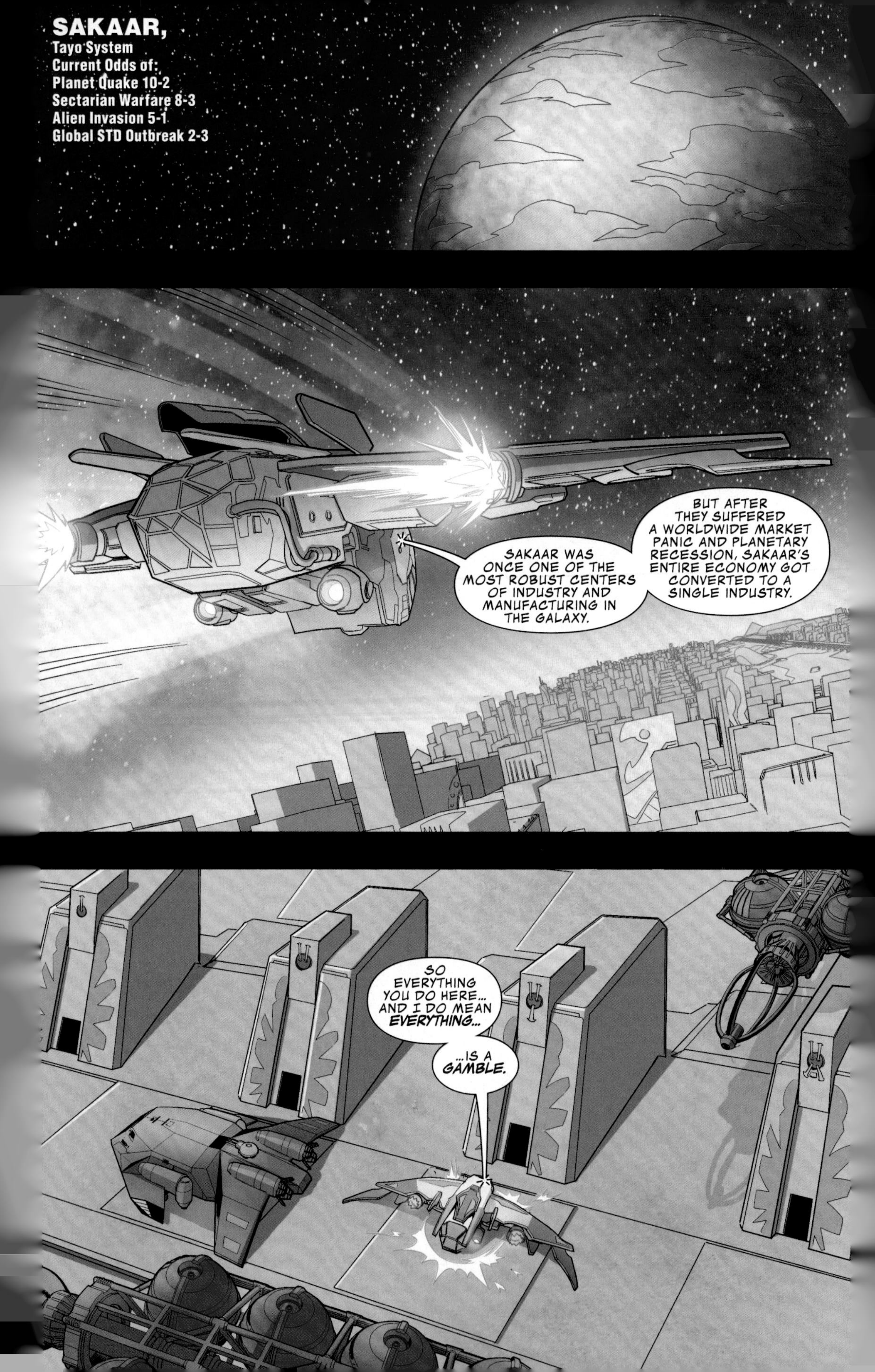
SAKAAR,
Tayo System
Current Odds of:
Planet Quake 10-2
Sectarian Warfare 8-3
Alien Invasion 5-1
Global STD Outbreak 2-3
SAKAAR WAS ONCE ONE OF THE MOST ROBUST CENTERS OF INDUSTRY AND MANUFACTURING IN THE GALAXY.
BUT AFTER THEY SUFFERED A WORLDWIDE MARKET PANIC AND PLANETARY RECESSION, SAKAAR'S ENTIRE ECONOMY GOT CONVERTED TO A SINGLE INDUSTRY.
SO EVERYTHING YOU DO HERE... AND I DO MEAN EVERYTHING...
...IS A GAMBLE.

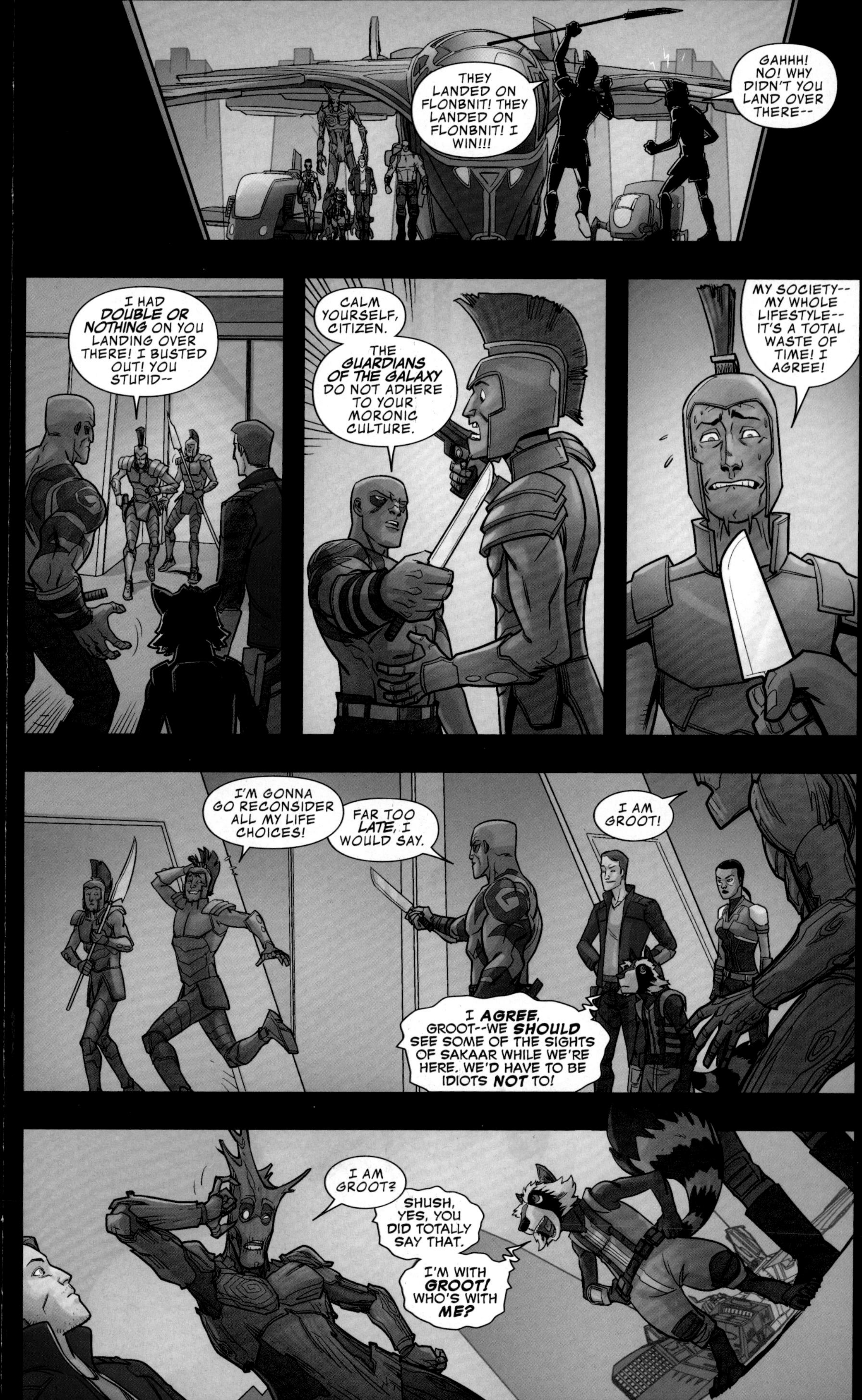
THEY LANDED ON FLONBNIT! THEY LANDED ON FLONBNIT! I WIN!!!
GAHHH! NO! WHY DIDN'T YOU LAND OVER THERE--
I HAD DOUBLE OR NOTHING ON YOU LANDING OVER THERE! I BUSTED OUT! YOU STUPID--
CALM YOURSELF, CITIZEN.
THE GUARDIANS OF THE GALAXY DO NOT ADHERE TO YOUR MORONIC CULTURE.
MY SOCIETY-- MY WHOLE LIFESTYLE-- IT'S A TOTAL WASTE OF TIME! I AGREE!
I'M GONNA GO RECONSIDER ALL MY LIFE CHOICES!
FAR TOO LATE, I WOULD SAY.
I AM GROOT!
I AGREE, GROOT--WE SHOULD SEE SOME OF THE SIGHTS OF SAKAAR WHILE WE'RE HERE. WE'D HAVE TO BE IDIOTS NOT TO!
I AM GROOT?
SHUSH, YES, YOU DID TOTALLY SAY THAT.
I'M WITH GROOT! WHO'S WITH ME?

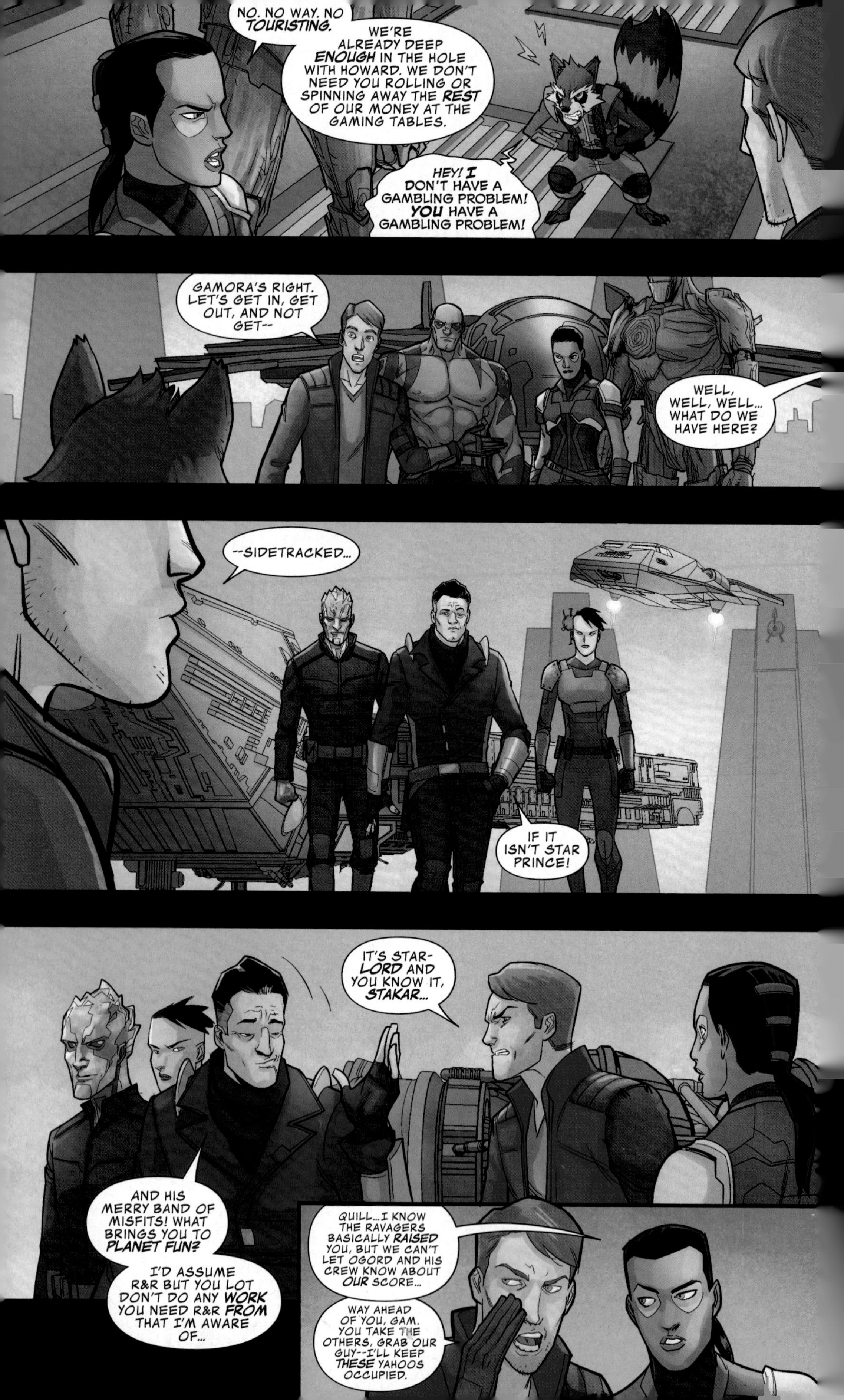
NO. NO WAY. NO TOURISTING.
WE'RE ALREADY DEEP ENOUGH IN THE HOLE WITH HOWARD. WE DON'T NEED YOU ROLLING OR SPINNING AWAY THE REST OF OUR MONEY AT THE GAMING TABLES.
HEY! I DON'T HAVE A GAMBLING PROBLEM! YOU HAVE A GAMBLING PROBLEM!
GAMORA'S RIGHT. LET'S GET IN, GET OUT, AND NOT GET--
WELL, WELL, WELL... WHAT DO WE HAVE HERE?
--SIDETRACKED...
IF IT ISN'T STAR PRINCE!
IT'S STAR-LORD AND YOU KNOW IT, STAKAR...
AND HIS MERRY BAND OF MISFITS! WHAT BRINGS YOU TO PLANET FUN?
I'D ASSUME R&R BUT YOU LOT DON'T DO ANY WORK YOU NEED R&R FROM THAT I'M AWARE OF...
QUILL...I KNOW THE RAVAGERS BASICALLY RAISED YOU, BUT WE CAN'T LET OGORD AND HIS CREW KNOW ABOUT OUR SCORE...
WAY AHEAD OF YOU, GAM. YOU TAKE THE OTHERS, GRAB OUR GUY--I'LL KEEP THESE YAHOOS OCCUPIED.

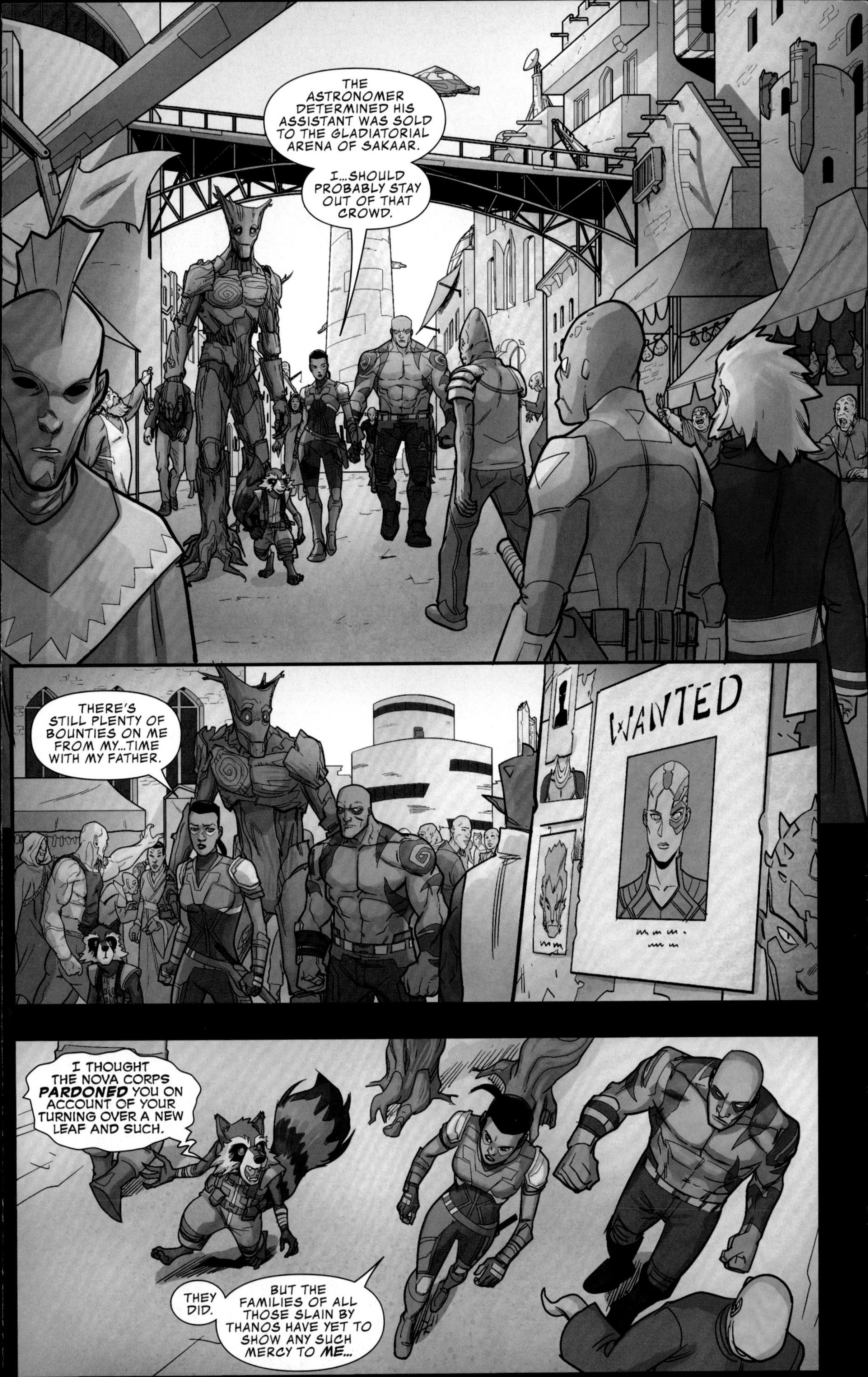
THE ASTRONOMER DETERMINED HIS ASSISTANT WAS SOLD TO THE GLADIATORIAL ARENA OF SAKAAR.
I...SHOULD PROBABLY STAY OUT OF THAT CROWD.
THERE'S STILL PLENTY OF BOUNTIES ON ME FROM MY...TIME WITH MY FATHER.
WANTED
I THOUGHT THE NOVA CORPS PARDONED YOU ON ACCOUNT OF YOUR TURNING OVER A NEW LEAF AND SUCH.
THEY DID.
BUT THE FAMILIES OF ALL THOSE SLAIN BY THANOS HAVE YET TO SHOW ANY SUCH MERCY TO ME...

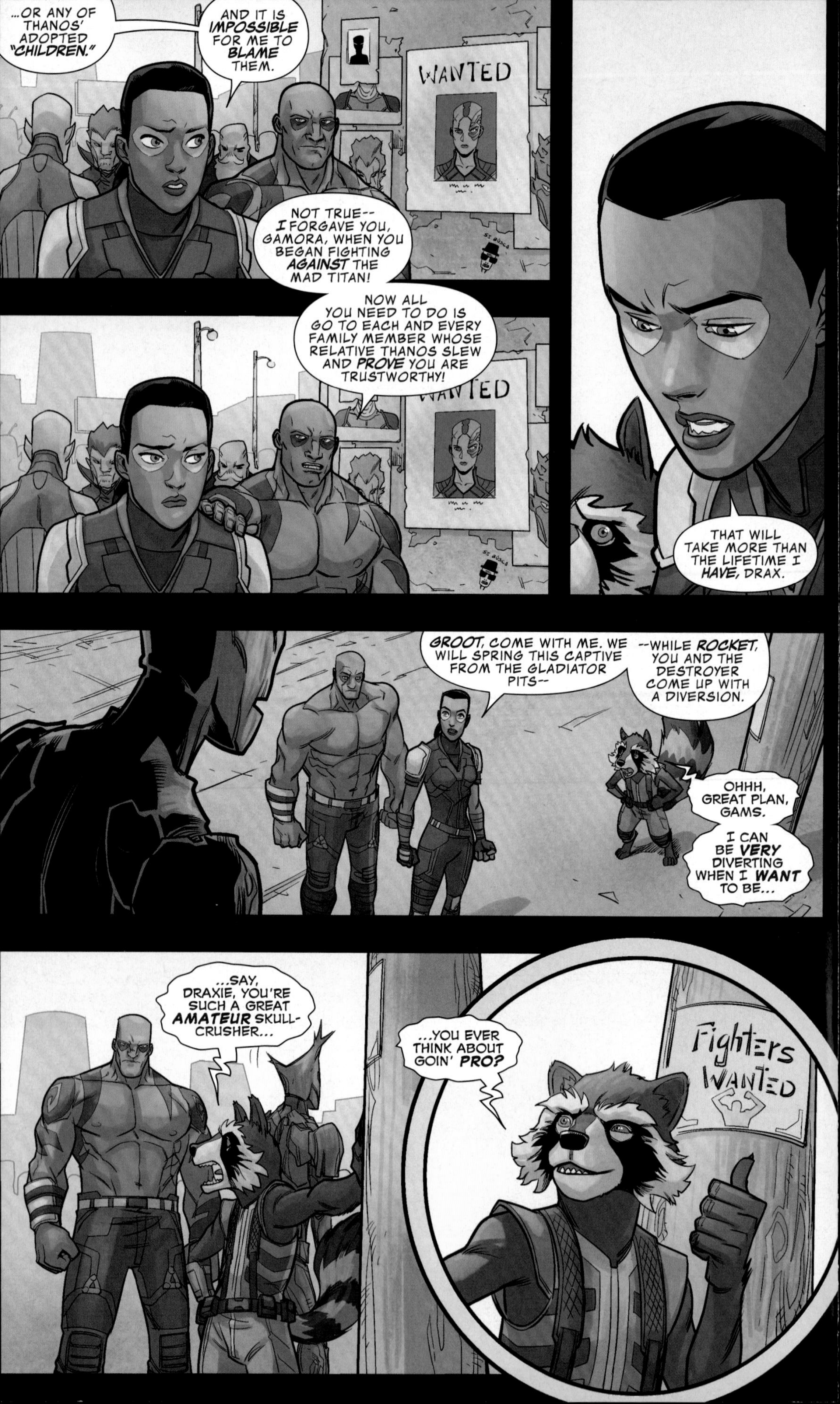
...OR ANY OF THANOS' ADOPTED "CHILDREN."
AND IT IS IMPOSSIBLE FOR ME TO BLAME THEM.
WANTED
NOT TRUE-- I FORGAVE YOU, GAMORA, WHEN YOU BEGAN FIGHTING AGAINST THE MAD TITAN!
NOW ALL YOU NEED TO DO IS GO TO EACH AND EVERY FAMILY MEMBER WHOSE RELATIVE THANOS SLEW AND PROVE YOU ARE TRUSTWORTHY!
THAT WILL TAKE MORE THAN THE LIFETIME I HAVE, DRAX.
GROOT, COME WITH ME. WE WILL SPRING THIS CAPTIVE FROM THE GLADIATOR PITS--
--WHILE ROCKET, YOU AND THE DESTROYER COME UP WITH A DIVERSION.
OHHH, GREAT PLAN, GAMS.
I CAN BE VERY DIVERTING WHEN I WANT TO BE...
...SAY, DRAXIE, YOU'RE SUCH A GREAT AMATEUR SKULL-CRUSHER...
...YOU EVER THINK ABOUT GOIN' PRO?
Fighters WANTED

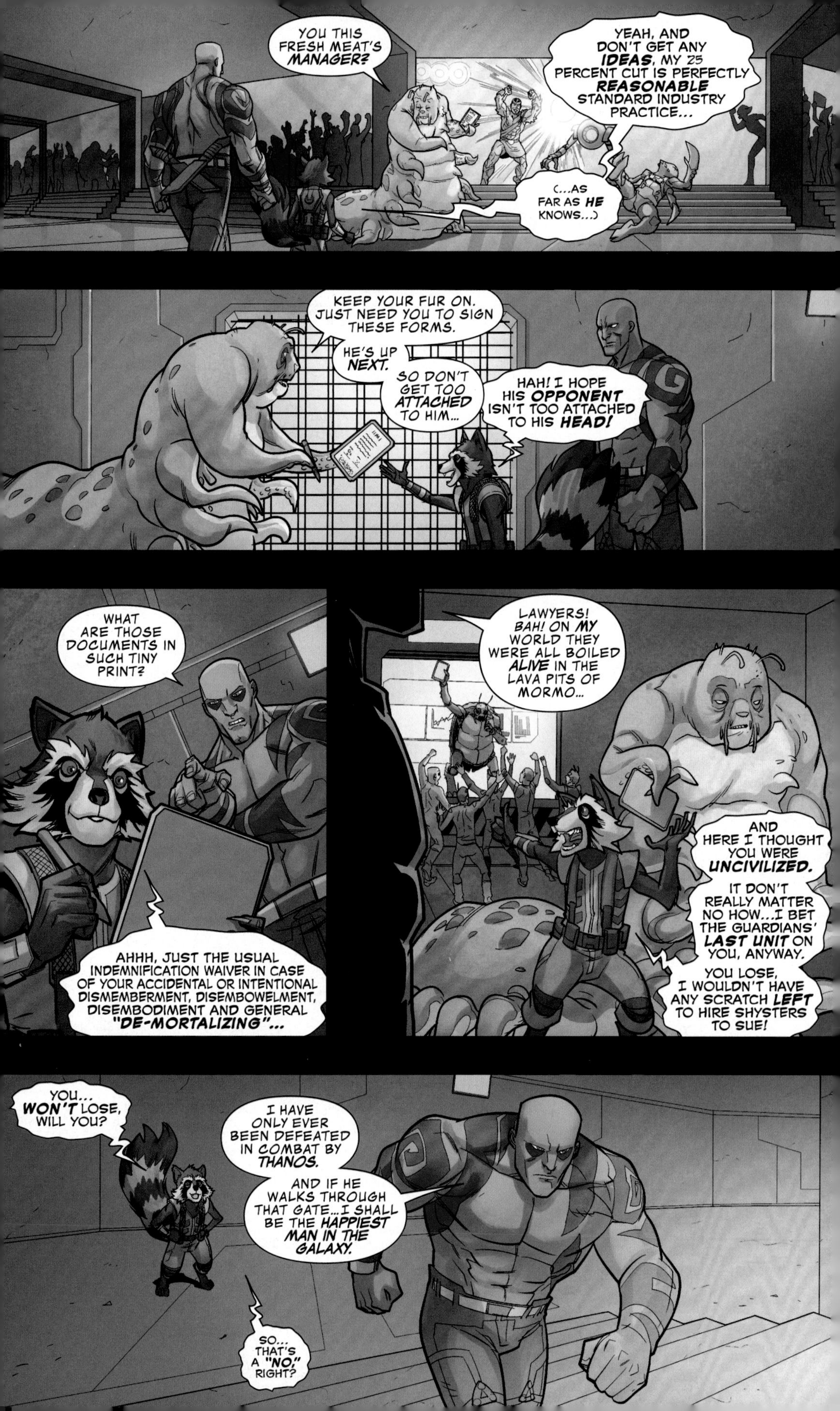
YOU THIS FRESH MEAT'S *MANAGER?*
YEAH, AND DON'T GET ANY *IDEAS*, MY 25 PERCENT CUT IS PERFECTLY *REASONABLE* STANDARD INDUSTRY PRACTICE...
(...AS FAR AS *HE* KNOWS...)
KEEP YOUR FUR ON. JUST NEED YOU TO SIGN THESE FORMS.
HE'S UP *NEXT*.
SO DON'T GET TOO *ATTACHED* TO HIM...
HAH! I HOPE HIS *OPPONENT* ISN'T TOO ATTACHED TO HIS *HEAD!*
WHAT ARE THOSE DOCUMENTS IN SUCH TINY PRINT?
AHHH, JUST THE USUAL INDEMNIFICATION WAIVER IN CASE OF YOUR ACCIDENTAL OR INTENTIONAL DISMEMBERMENT, DISEMBOWELMENT, DISEMBODIMENT AND GENERAL *"DE-MORTALIZING"...*
LAWYERS! BAH! ON *MY* WORLD THEY WERE ALL BOILED *ALIVE* IN THE LAVA PITS OF MORMO...
AND HERE I THOUGHT YOU WERE *UNCIVILIZED.*
IT DON'T REALLY MATTER NO HOW...I BET THE GUARDIANS' *LAST UNIT* ON YOU, ANYWAY.
YOU LOSE, I WOULDN'T HAVE ANY SCRATCH *LEFT* TO HIRE SHYSTERS TO SUE!
YOU... *WON'T* LOSE, WILL YOU?
I HAVE ONLY EVER BEEN DEFEATED IN COMBAT BY *THANOS.*
AND IF HE WALKS THROUGH THAT GATE...I SHALL BE THE *HAPPIEST MAN IN THE GALAXY.*
SO... THAT'S A *"NO,"* RIGHT?

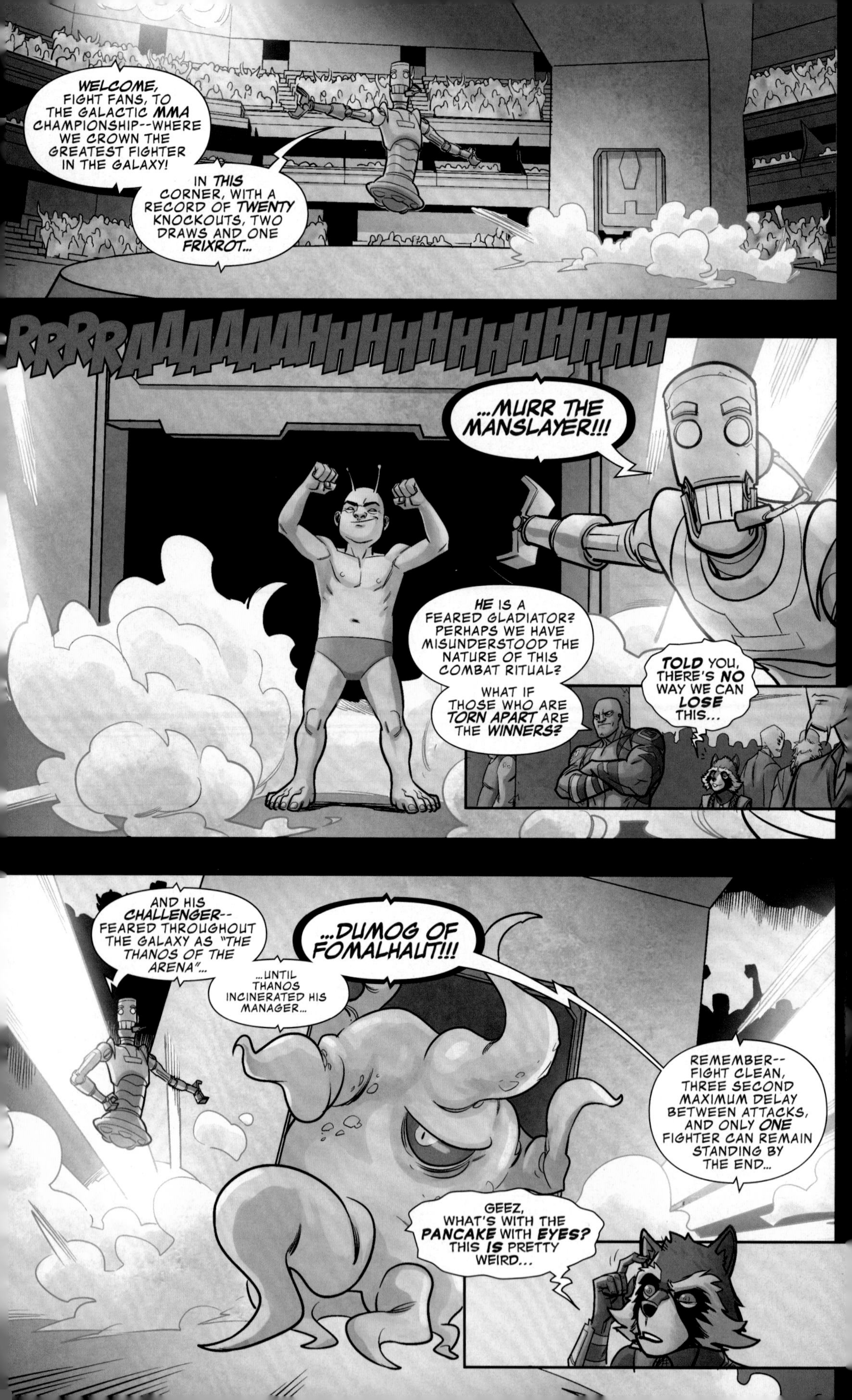
WELCOME, FIGHT FANS, TO THE GALACTIC MMA CHAMPIONSHIP--WHERE WE CROWN THE GREATEST FIGHTER IN THE GALAXY!
IN THIS CORNER, WITH A RECORD OF TWENTY KNOCKOUTS, TWO DRAWS AND ONE FRIXROT...
RRRRAAAAAAHHHHHHHHHHHH
...MURR THE MANSLAYER!!!
HE IS A FEARED GLADIATOR? PERHAPS WE HAVE MISUNDERSTOOD THE NATURE OF THIS COMBAT RITUAL?
WHAT IF THOSE WHO ARE TORN APART ARE THE WINNERS?
TOLD YOU, THERE'S NO WAY WE CAN LOSE THIS...
AND HIS CHALLENGER-- FEARED THROUGHOUT THE GALAXY AS "THE THANOS OF THE ARENA"...
...UNTIL THANOS INCINERATED HIS MANAGER...
...DUMOG OF FOMALHAUT!!!
REMEMBER-- FIGHT CLEAN, THREE SECOND MAXIMUM DELAY BETWEEN ATTACKS, AND ONLY ONE FIGHTER CAN REMAIN STANDING BY THE END...
GEEZ, WHAT'S WITH THE PANCAKE WITH EYES? THIS IS PRETTY WEIRD...

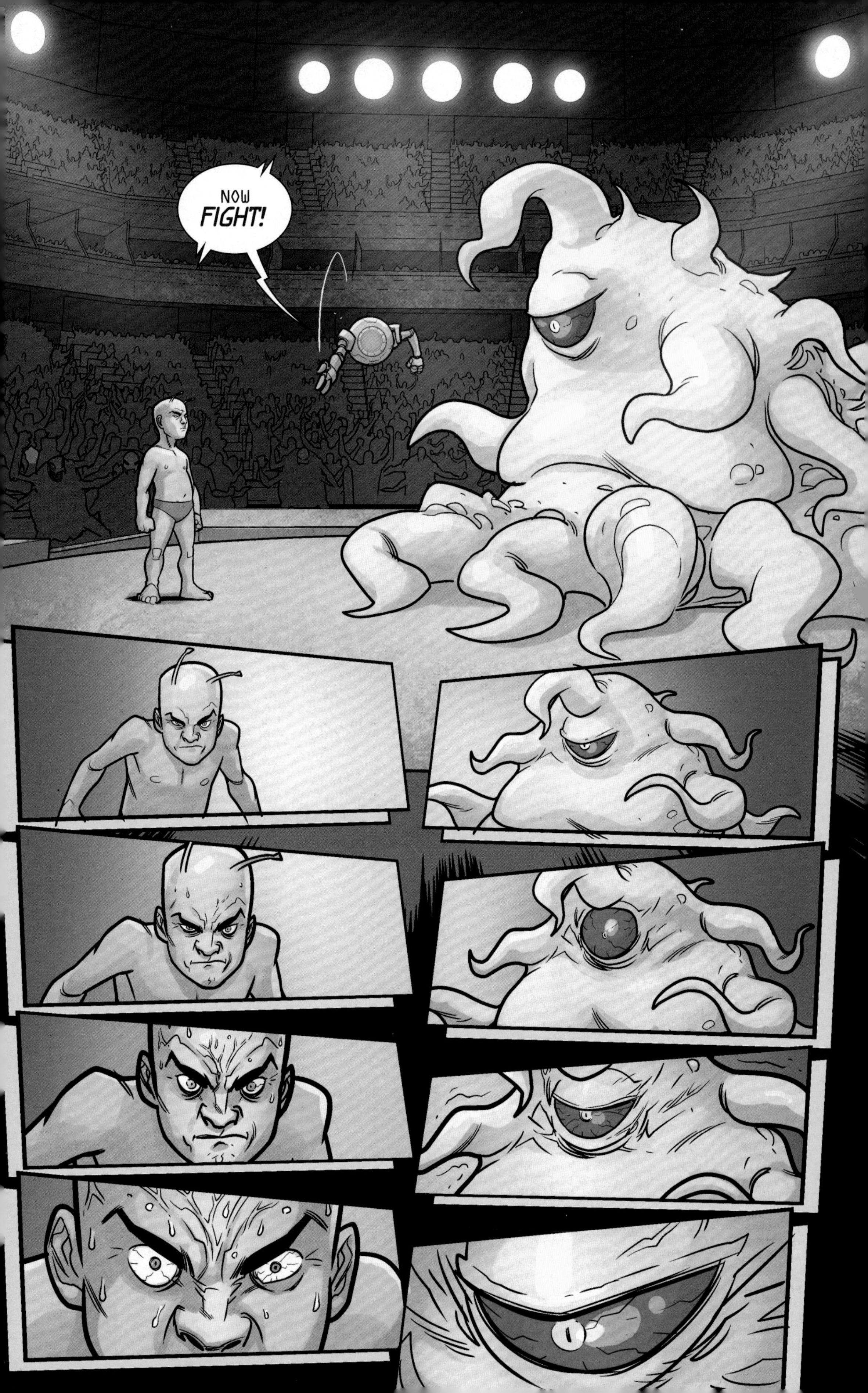
NOW FIGHT!

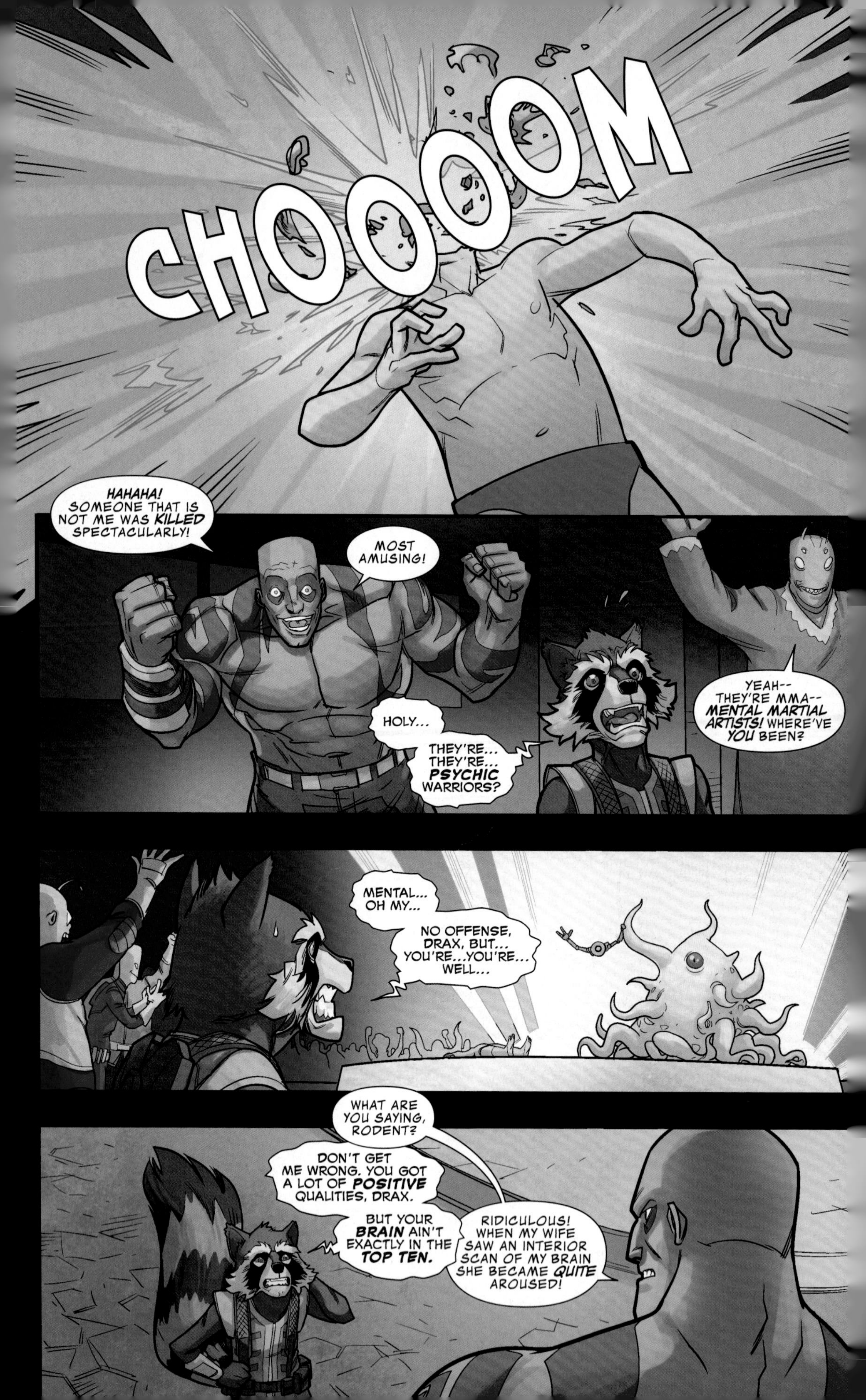
CHOOOOM
HAHAHA! SOMEONE THAT IS NOT ME WAS KILLED SPECTACULARLY!
MOST AMUSING!
HOLY...
THEY'RE... THEY'RE... PSYCHIC WARRIORS?
YEAH-- THEY'RE MMA-- MENTAL MARTIAL ARTISTS! WHERE'VE YOU BEEN?
MENTAL... OH MY...
NO OFFENSE, DRAX, BUT... YOU'RE...YOU'RE... WELL...
WHAT ARE YOU SAYING, RODENT?
DON'T GET ME WRONG. YOU GOT A LOT OF POSITIVE QUALITIES, DRAX.
BUT YOUR BRAIN AIN'T EXACTLY IN THE TOP TEN.
RIDICULOUS! WHEN MY WIFE SAW AN INTERIOR SCAN OF MY BRAIN SHE BECAME QUITE AROUSED!

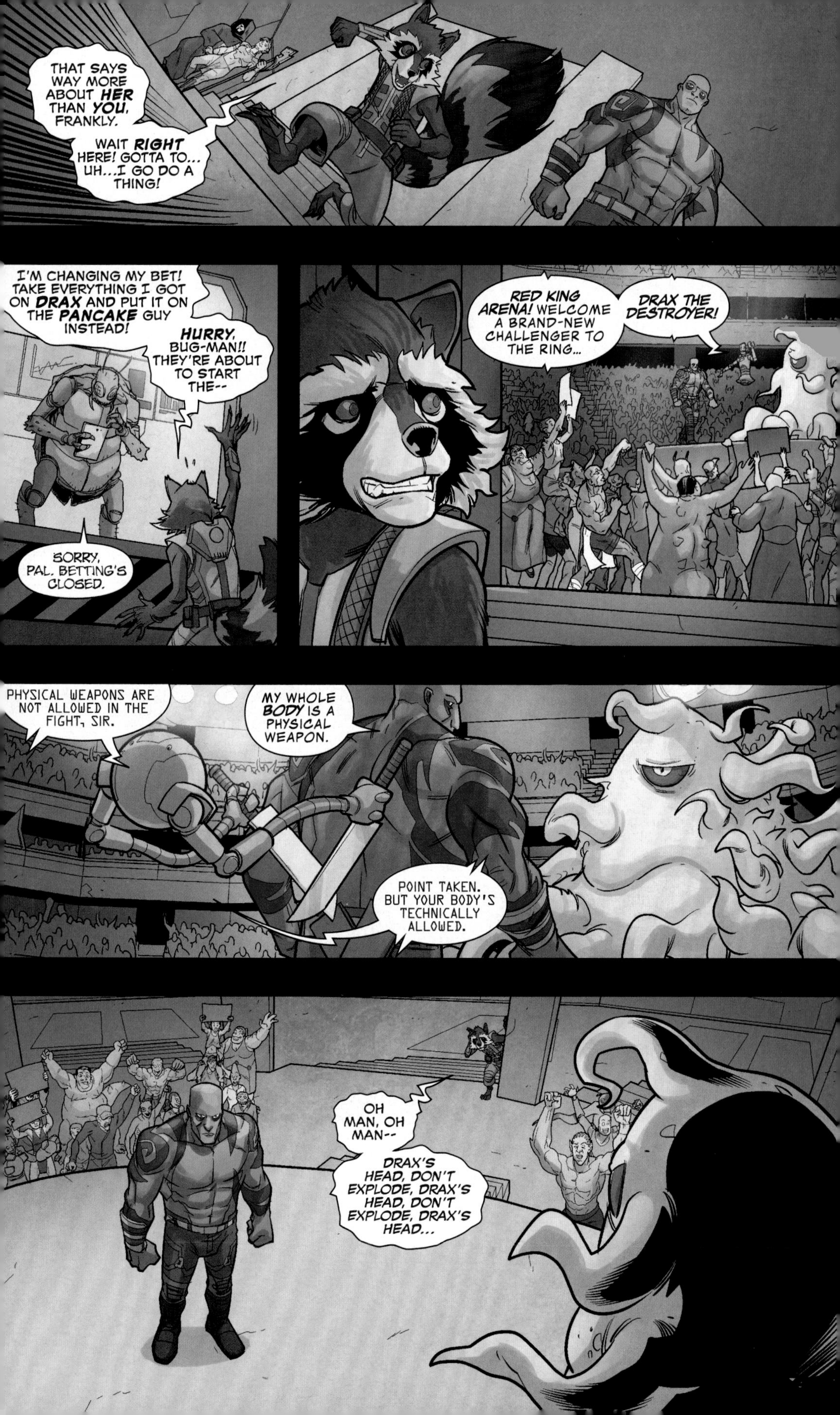
THAT SAYS WAY MORE ABOUT HER THAN YOU, FRANKLY.
WAIT RIGHT HERE! GOTTA TO... UH...I GO DO A THING!
I'M CHANGING MY BET! TAKE EVERYTHING I GOT ON DRAX AND PUT IT ON THE PANCAKE GUY INSTEAD!
HURRY, BUG-MAN!! THEY'RE ABOUT TO START THE--
SORRY, PAL. BETTING'S CLOSED.
RED KING ARENA! WELCOME A BRAND-NEW CHALLENGER TO THE RING...
DRAX THE DESTROYER!
PHYSICAL WEAPONS ARE NOT ALLOWED IN THE FIGHT, SIR.
MY WHOLE BODY IS A PHYSICAL WEAPON.
POINT TAKEN. BUT YOUR BODY'S TECHNICALLY ALLOWED.
OH MAN, OH MAN--
DRAX'S HEAD, DON'T EXPLODE, DRAX'S HEAD, DON'T EXPLODE, DRAX'S HEAD...

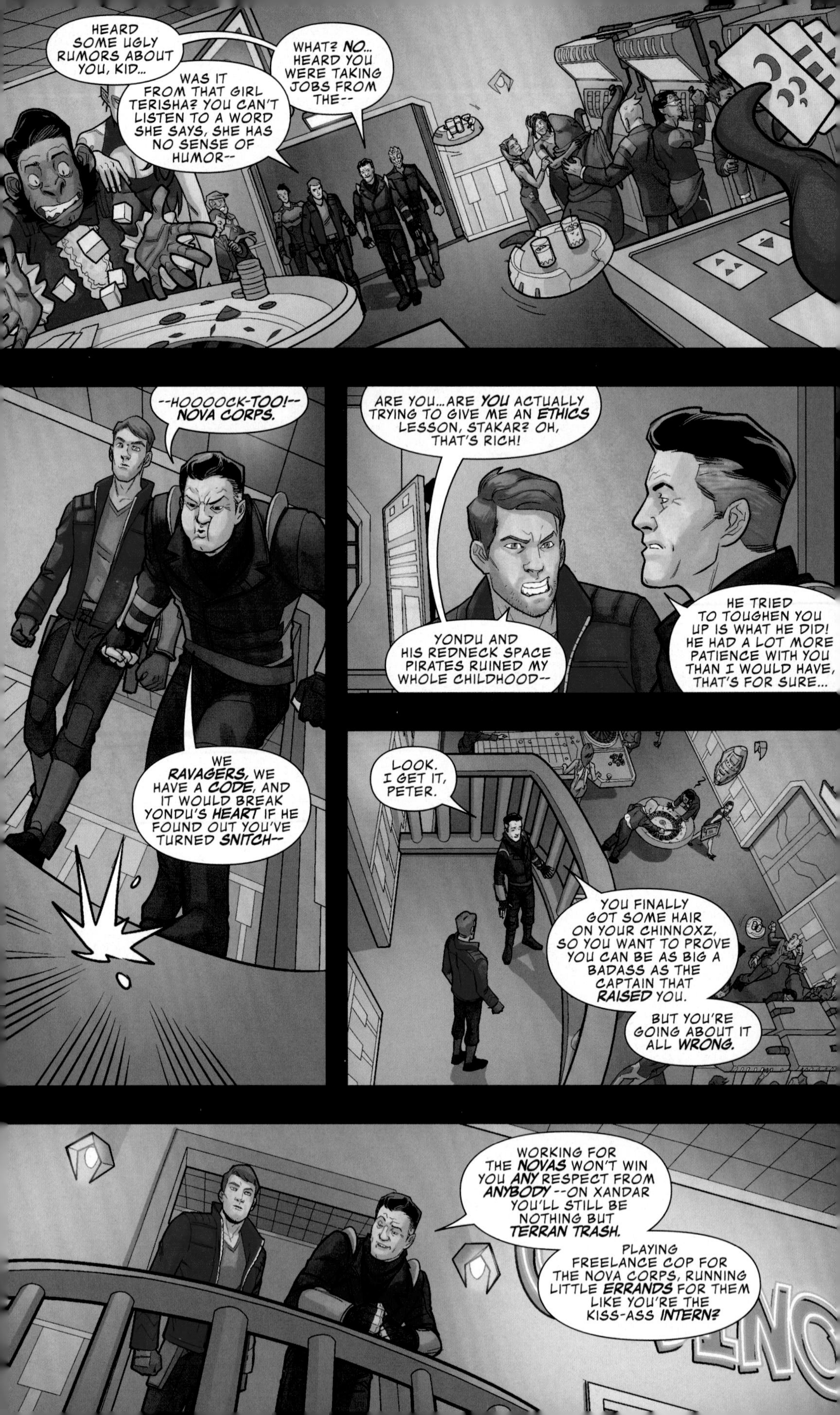
HEARD SOME UGLY RUMORS ABOUT YOU, KID...
WAS IT FROM THAT GIRL TERISHA? YOU CAN'T LISTEN TO A WORD SHE SAYS, SHE HAS NO SENSE OF HUMOR--
WHAT? NO... HEARD YOU WERE TAKING JOBS FROM THE--
--HOOOOCK-TOO!-- NOVA CORPS.
WE RAVAGERS, WE HAVE A CODE, AND IT WOULD BREAK YONDU'S HEART IF HE FOUND OUT YOU'VE TURNED SNITCH--
ARE YOU...ARE YOU ACTUALLY TRYING TO GIVE ME AN ETHICS LESSON, STAKAR? OH, THAT'S RICH!
YONDU AND HIS REDNECK SPACE PIRATES RUINED MY WHOLE CHILDHOOD--
HE TRIED TO TOUGHEN YOU UP IS WHAT HE DID! HE HAD A LOT MORE PATIENCE WITH YOU THAN I WOULD HAVE, THAT'S FOR SURE...
LOOK. I GET IT, PETER.
YOU FINALLY GOT SOME HAIR ON YOUR CHINNOXZ, SO YOU WANT TO PROVE YOU CAN BE AS BIG A BADASS AS THE CAPTAIN THAT RAISED YOU.
BUT YOU'RE GOING ABOUT IT ALL WRONG.
WORKING FOR THE NOVAS WON'T WIN YOU ANY RESPECT FROM ANYBODY --ON XANDAR YOU'LL STILL BE NOTHING BUT TERRAN TRASH.
PLAYING FREELANCE COP FOR THE NOVA CORPS, RUNNING LITTLE ERRANDS FOR THEM LIKE YOU'RE THE KISS-ASS INTERN?

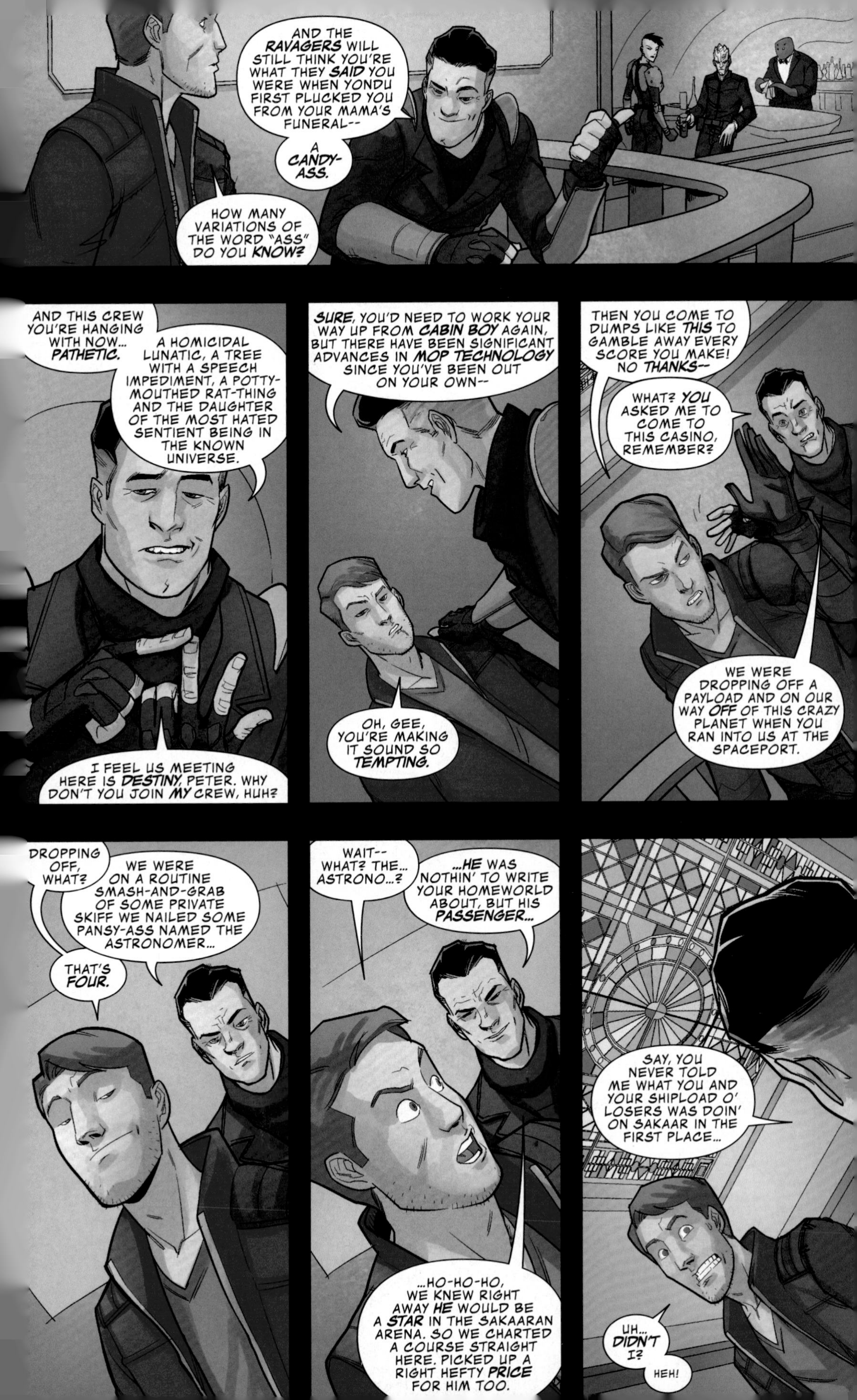
AND THE RAVAGERS WILL STILL THINK YOU'RE WHAT THEY SAID YOU WERE WHEN YONDU FIRST PLUCKED YOU FROM YOUR MAMA'S FUNERAL--
A CANDY-ASS.
HOW MANY VARIATIONS OF THE WORD "ASS" DO YOU KNOW?
AND THIS CREW YOU'RE HANGING WITH NOW... PATHETIC.
A HOMICIDAL LUNATIC, A TREE WITH A SPEECH IMPEDIMENT, A POTTY-MOUTHED RAT-THING AND THE DAUGHTER OF THE MOST HATED SENTIENT BEING IN THE KNOWN UNIVERSE.
I FEEL US MEETING HERE IS DESTINY, PETER. WHY DON'T YOU JOIN MY CREW, HUH?
SURE, YOU'D NEED TO WORK YOUR WAY UP FROM CABIN BOY AGAIN, BUT THERE HAVE BEEN SIGNIFICANT ADVANCES IN MOP TECHNOLOGY SINCE YOU'VE BEEN OUT ON YOUR OWN--
OH, GEE, YOU'RE MAKING IT SOUND SO TEMPTING.
THEN YOU COME TO DUMPS LIKE THIS TO GAMBLE AWAY EVERY SCORE YOU MAKE! NO THANKS--
WHAT? YOU ASKED ME TO COME TO THIS CASINO, REMEMBER?
WE WERE DROPPING OFF A PAYLOAD AND ON OUR WAY OFF OF THIS CRAZY PLANET WHEN YOU RAN INTO US AT THE SPACEPORT.
DROPPING OFF, WHAT?
WE WERE ON A ROUTINE SMASH-AND-GRAB OF SOME PRIVATE SKIFF WE NAILED SOME PANSY-ASS NAMED THE ASTRONOMER...
THAT'S FOUR.
WAIT-- WHAT? THE... ASTRONO...?
...HE WAS NOTHIN' TO WRITE YOUR HOMEWORLD ABOUT, BUT HIS PASSENGER...
...HO-HO-HO, WE KNEW RIGHT AWAY HE WOULD BE A STAR IN THE SAKAARAN ARENA. SO WE CHARTED A COURSE STRAIGHT HERE. PICKED UP A RIGHT HEFTY PRICE FOR HIM TOO.
SAY, YOU NEVER TOLD ME WHAT YOU AND YOUR SHIPLOAD O' LOSERS WAS DOIN' ON SAKAAR IN THE FIRST PLACE...
UH... DIDN'T I?
HEH!

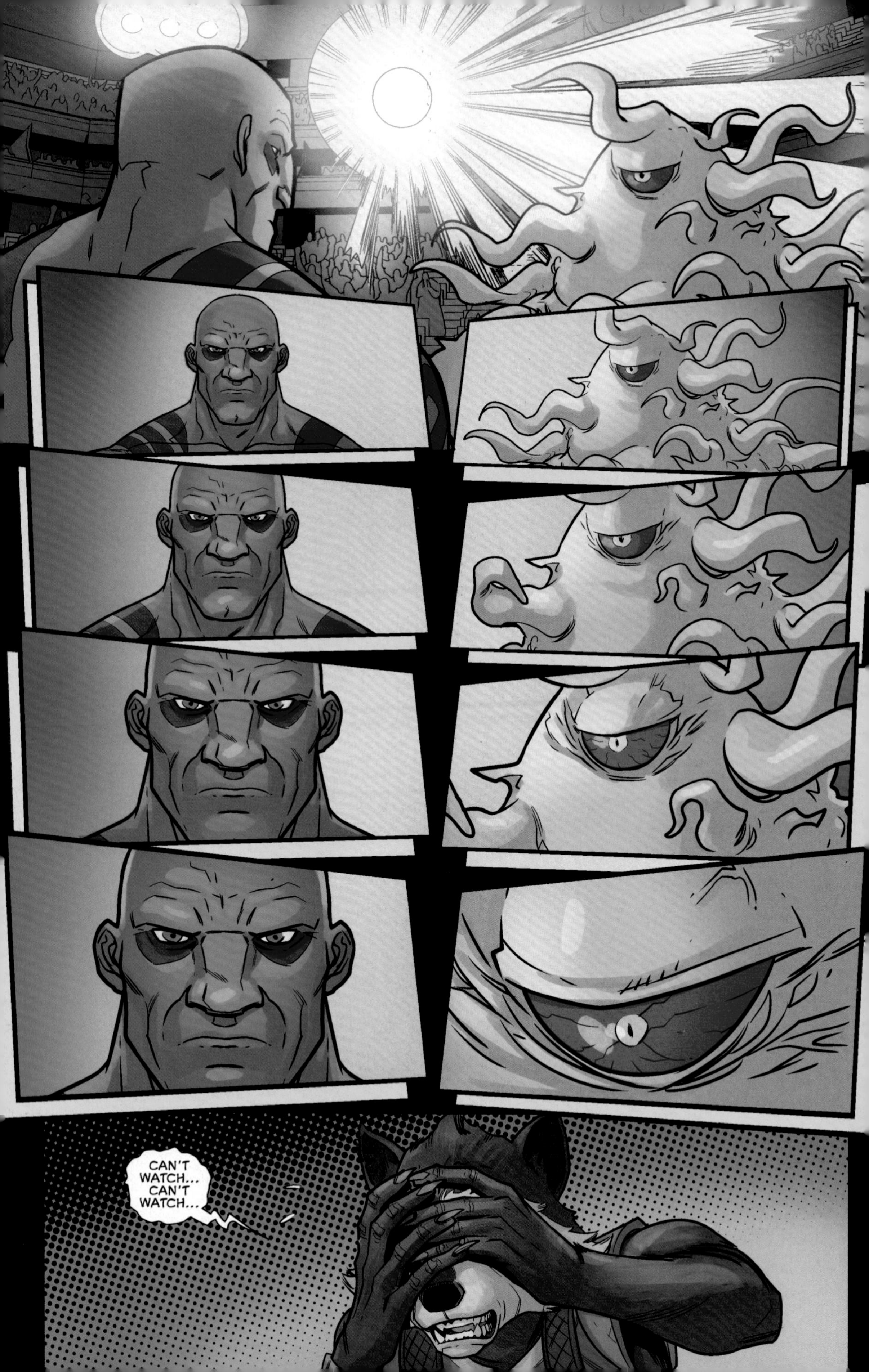
CAN'T WATCH... CAN'T WATCH...

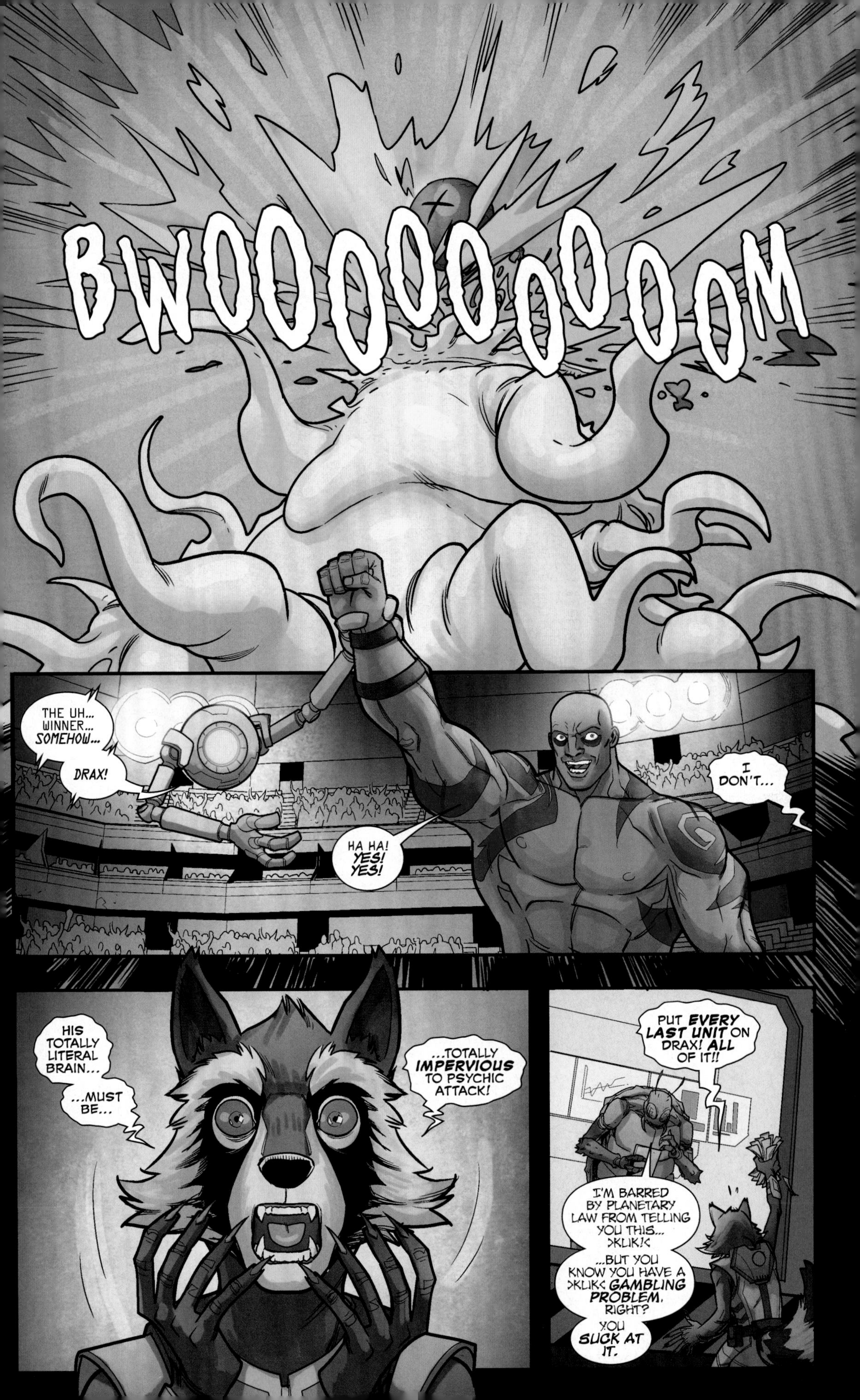
BWOOOOOOOOM
THE UH... WINNER... SOMEHOW...
DRAX!
I DON'T...
HA HA! YES! YES!
HIS TOTALLY LITERAL BRAIN...
...MUST BE...
...TOTALLY IMPERVIOUS TO PSYCHIC ATTACK!
PUT EVERY LAST UNIT ON DRAX! ALL OF IT!!
I'M BARRED BY PLANETARY LAW FROM TELLING YOU THIS... >KLIK<
...BUT YOU KNOW YOU HAVE A >KLIK< GAMBLING PROBLEM, RIGHT?
YOU SUCK AT IT.

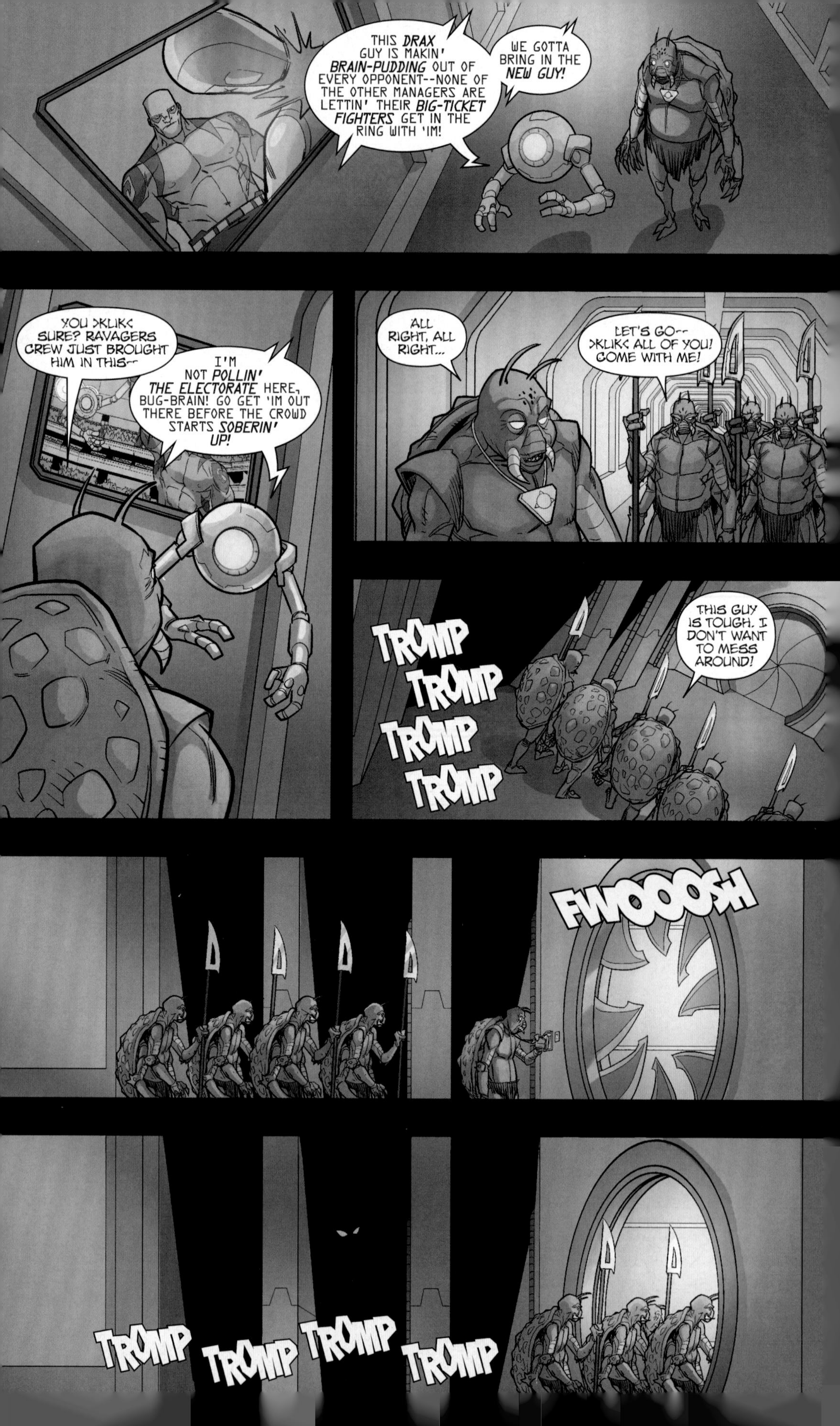

THIS DRAX GUY IS MAKIN' BRAIN-PUDDING OUT OF EVERY OPPONENT--NONE OF THE OTHER MANAGERS ARE LETTIN' THEIR BIG-TICKET FIGHTERS GET IN THE RING WITH 'IM!
WE GOTTA BRING IN THE NEW GUY!
YOU >KLIK< SURE? RAVAGERS CREW JUST BROUGHT HIM IN THIS--
I'M NOT POLLIN' THE ELECTORATE HERE, BUG-BRAIN! GO GET 'IM OUT THERE BEFORE THE CROWD STARTS SOBERIN' UP!
ALL RIGHT, ALL RIGHT...
LET'S GO-- >KLIK< ALL OF YOU! COME WITH ME!
TROMP TROMP TROMP TROMP
THIS GUY IS TOUGH. I DON'T WANT TO MESS AROUND!
FWOOOSH
TROMP TROMP TROMP TROMP

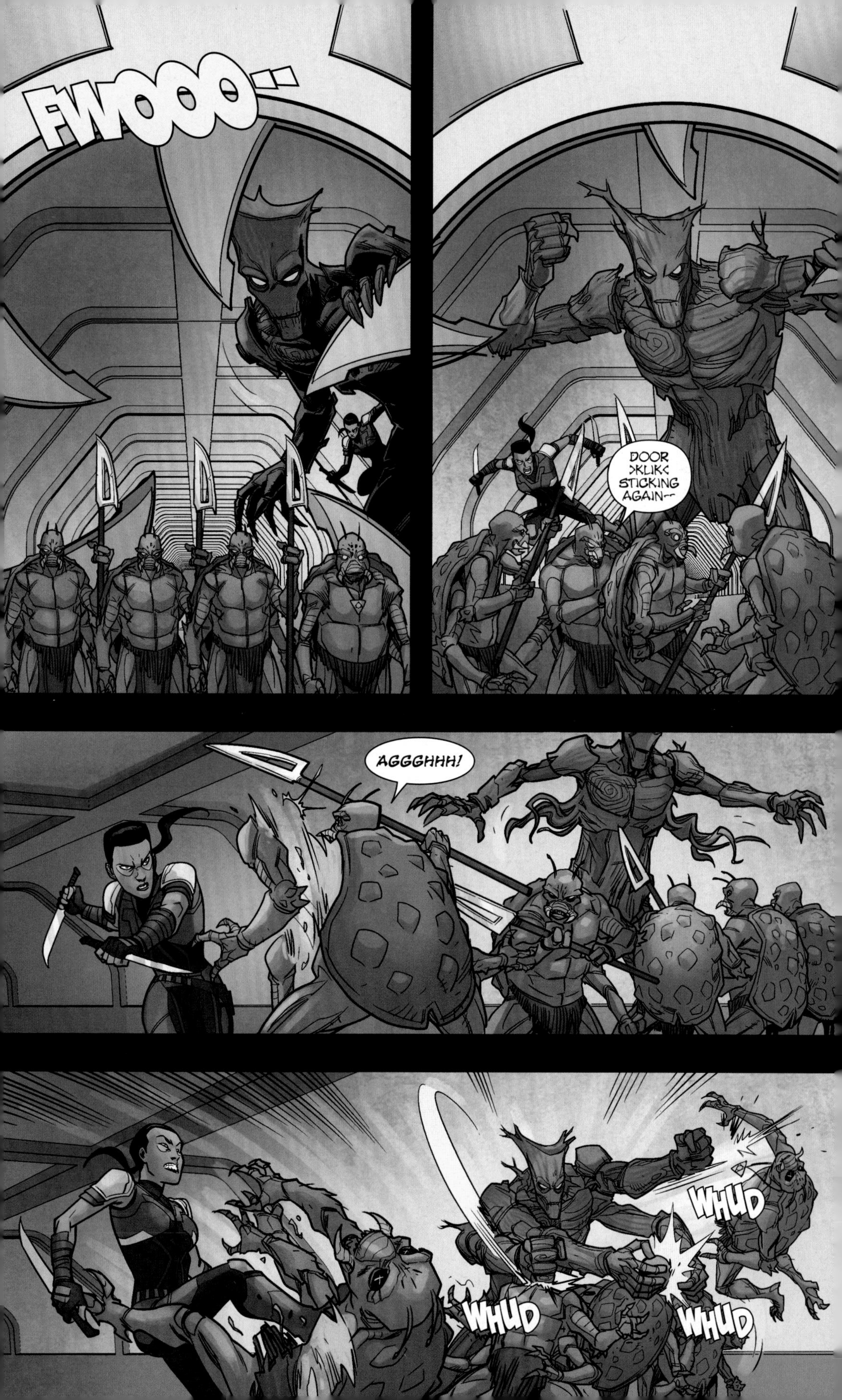
FWOOO--
DOOR >KLIK< STICKING AGAIN--
AGGGHHH!
WHUD
WHUD
WHUD

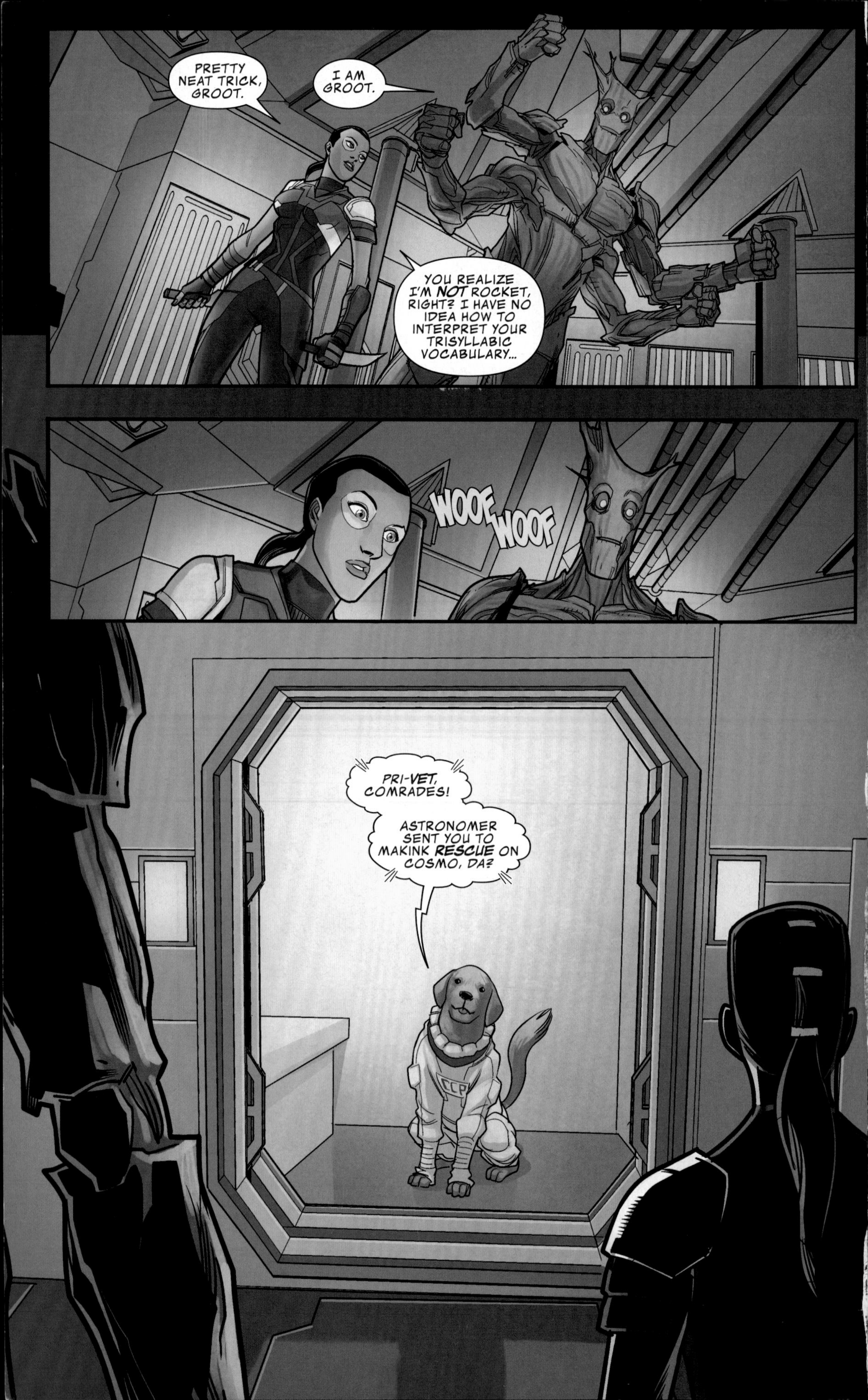
PRETTY NEAT TRICK, GROOT.
I AM GROOT.
YOU REALIZE I'M **NOT** ROCKET, RIGHT? I HAVE NO IDEA HOW TO INTERPRET YOUR TRISYLLABIC VOCABULARY...
WOOF WOOF
PRI-**VET**, COMRADES!
ASTRONOMER SENT YOU TO MAKINK **RESCUE** ON COSMO, DA?
CCP

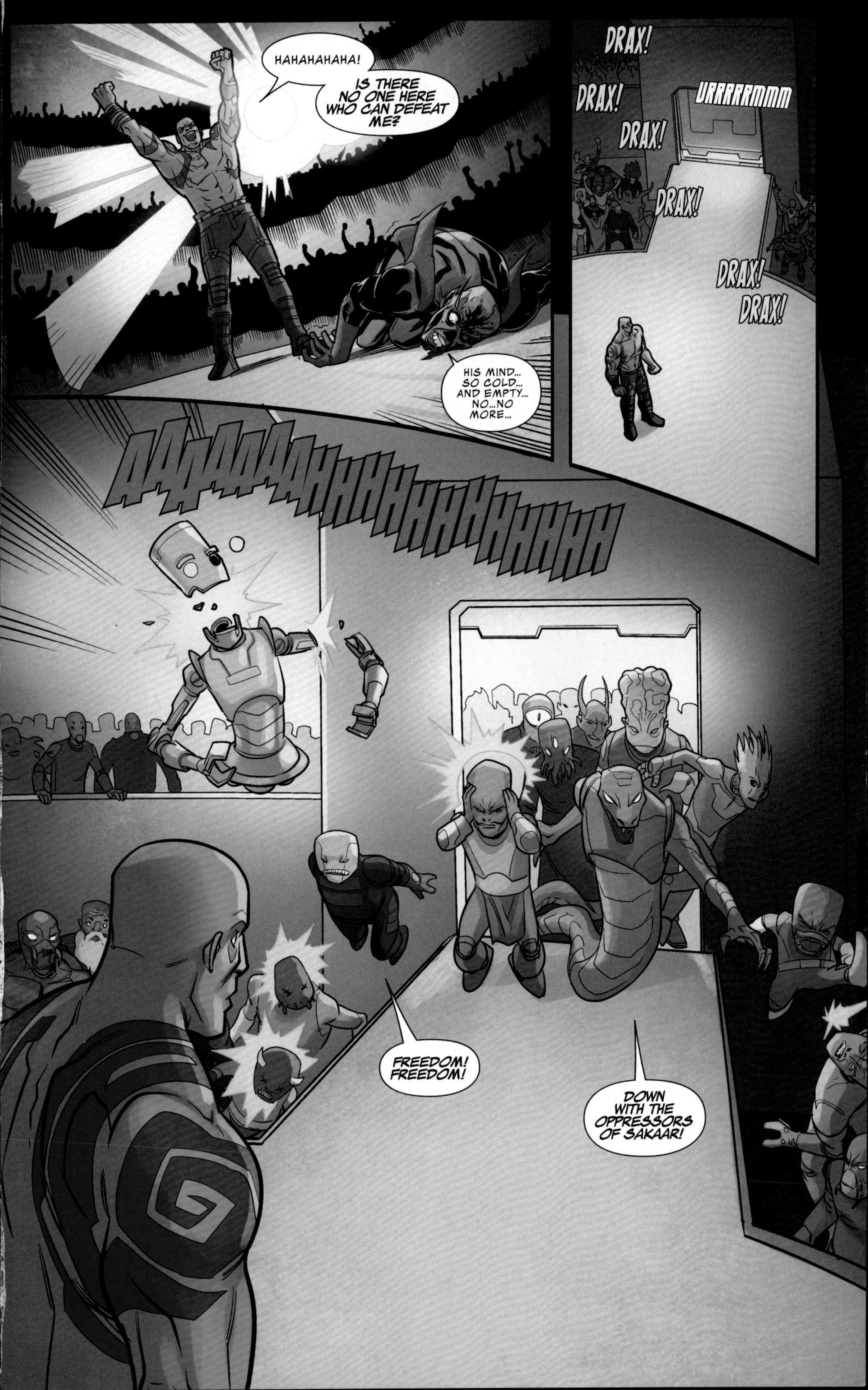
HAHAHAHAHA!
IS THERE NO ONE HERE WHO CAN DEFEAT ME?
HIS MIND... SO COLD... AND EMPTY... NO...NO MORE...
DRAX!
DRAX!
URRRRRMMM
DRAX!
DRAX!
DRAX!
DRAX!
AAAAAAAHHHHHHHHHHHHHH
FREEDOM! FREEDOM!
DOWN WITH THE OPPRESSORS OF SAKAAR!

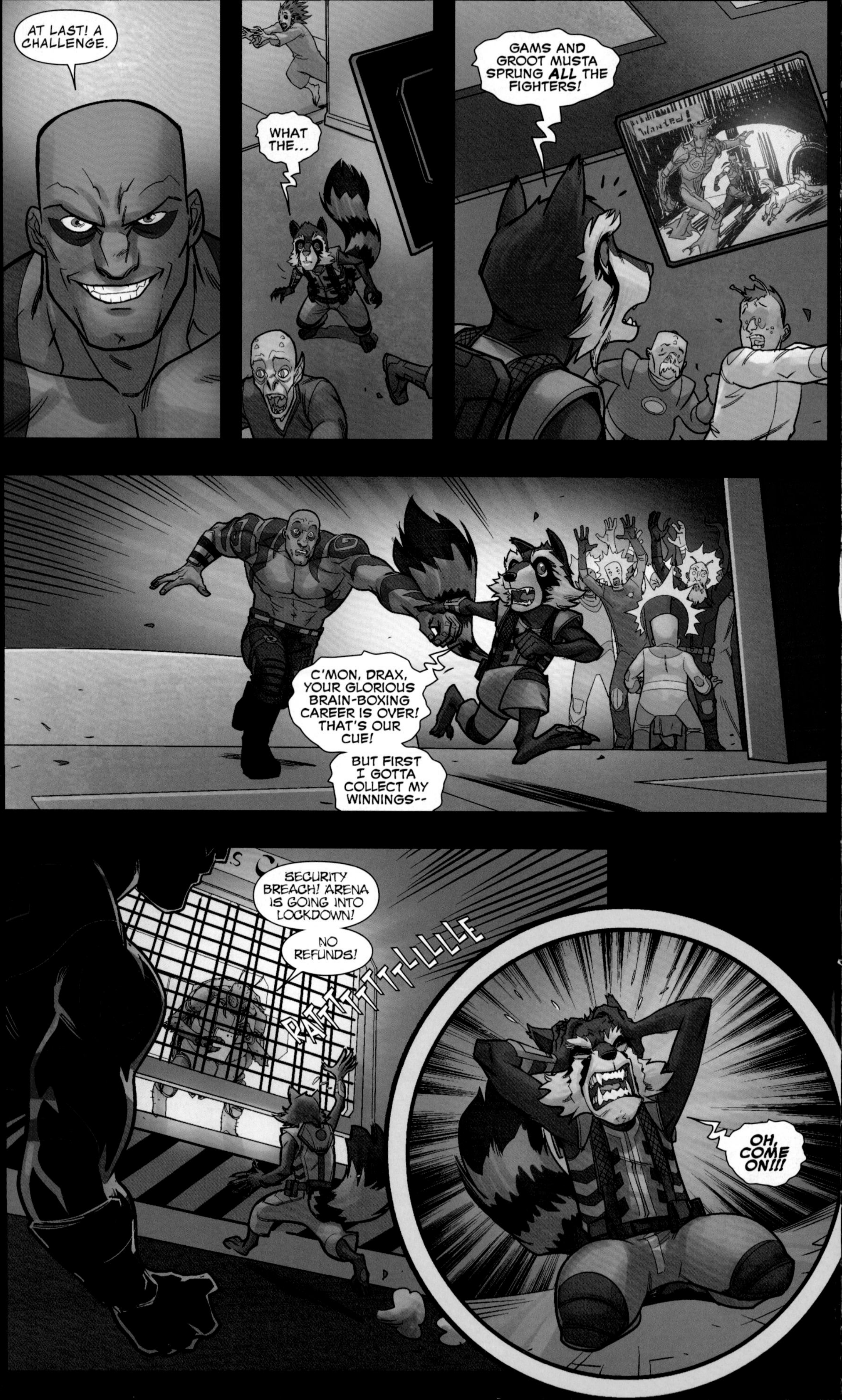
AT LAST! A CHALLENGE.
WHAT THE...
GAMS AND GROOT MUSTA SPRUNG ALL THE FIGHTERS!
Wanted!
C'MON, DRAX, YOUR GLORIOUS BRAIN-BOXING CAREER IS OVER! THAT'S OUR CUE!
BUT FIRST I GOTTA COLLECT MY WINNINGS--
SECURITY BREACH! ARENA IS GOING INTO LOCKDOWN!
NO REFUNDS!
RATTTTTTT-LLLLLE
OH, COME ON!!!

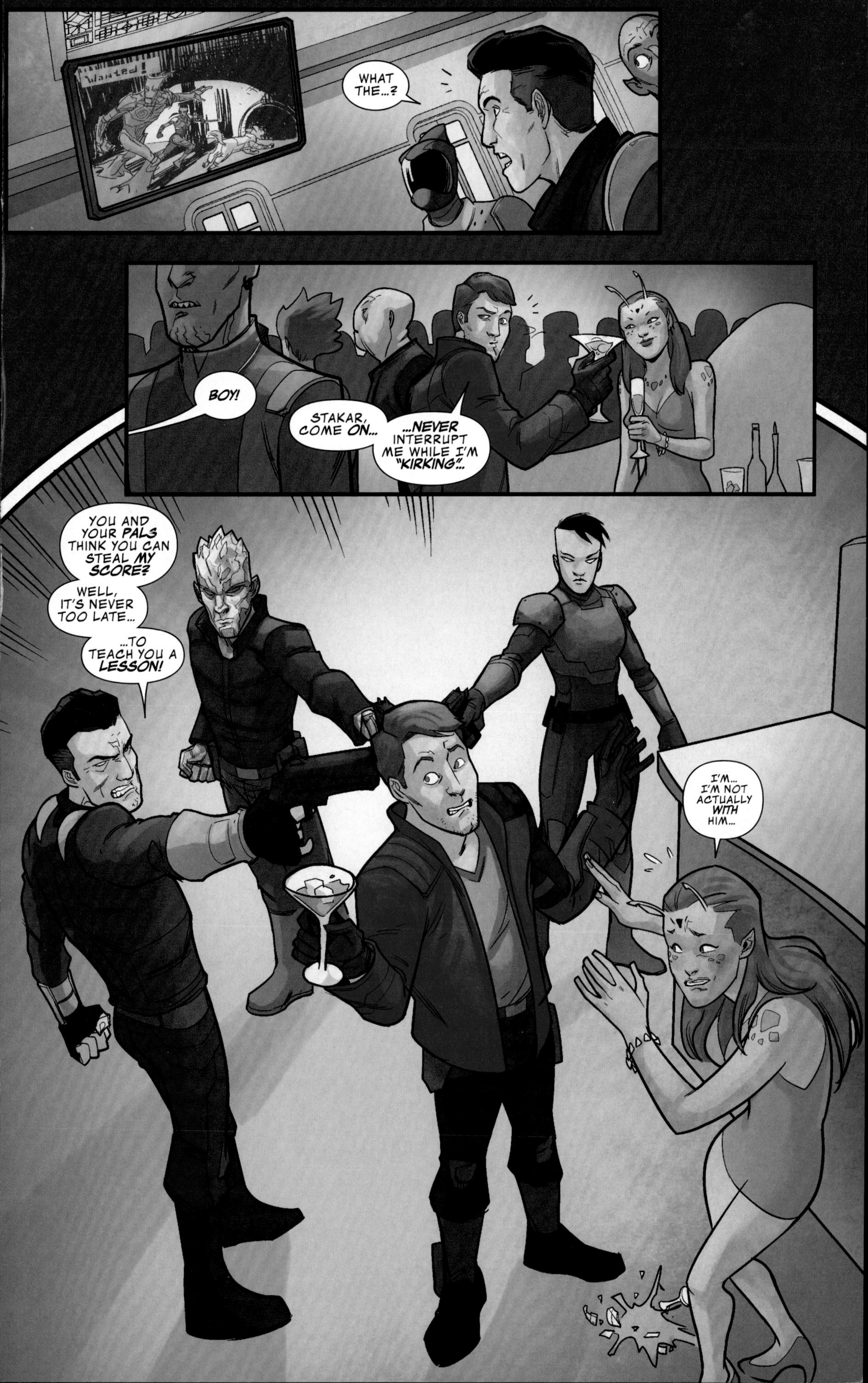

WHAT THE...?
BOY!
STAKAR, COME ON...
...NEVER INTERRUPT ME WHILE I'M "KIRKING"...
YOU AND YOUR PALS THINK YOU CAN STEAL MY SCORE?
WELL, IT'S NEVER TOO LATE...
...TO TEACH YOU A LESSON!
I'M... I'M NOT ACTUALLY WITH HIM...

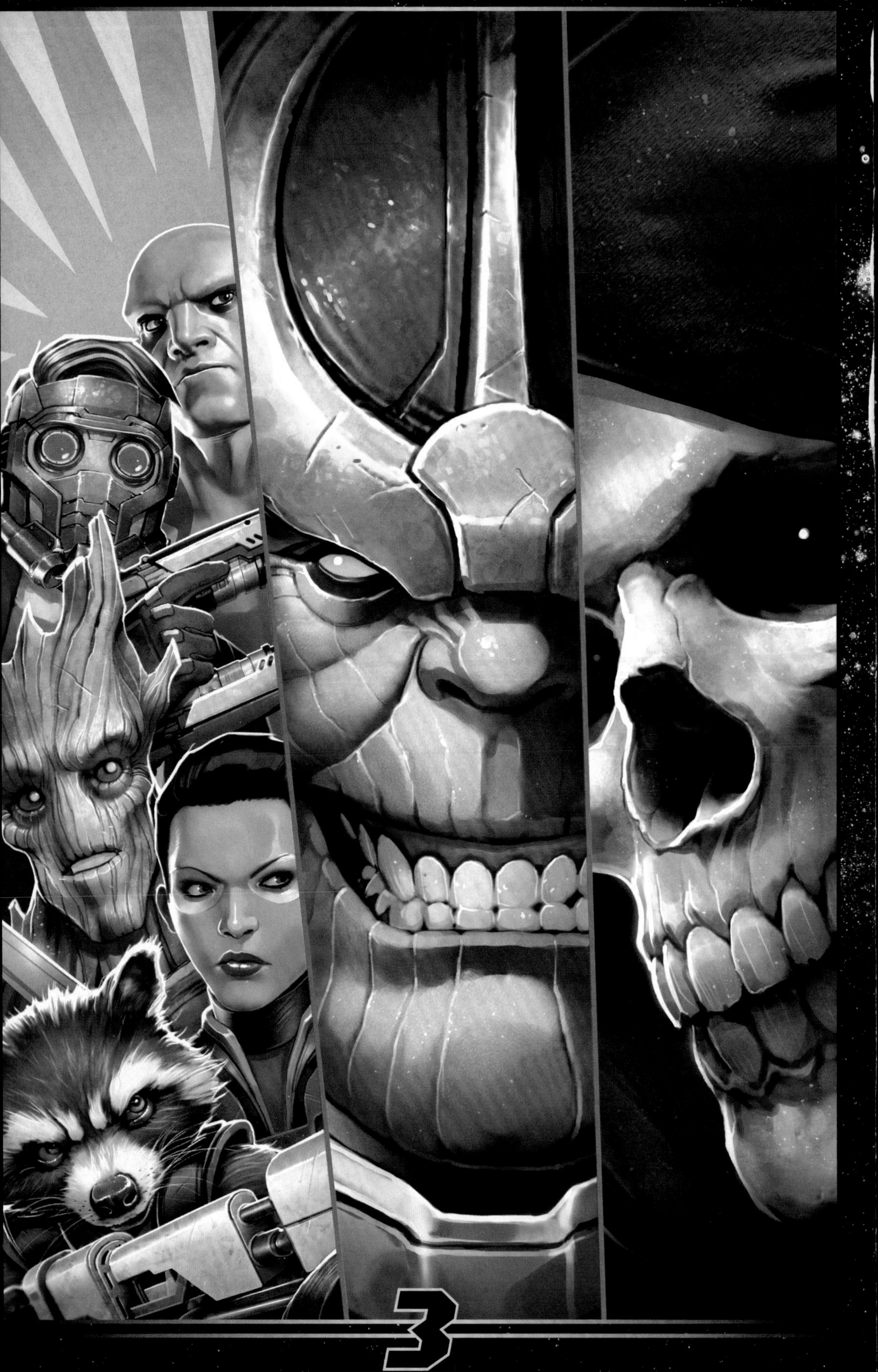
3

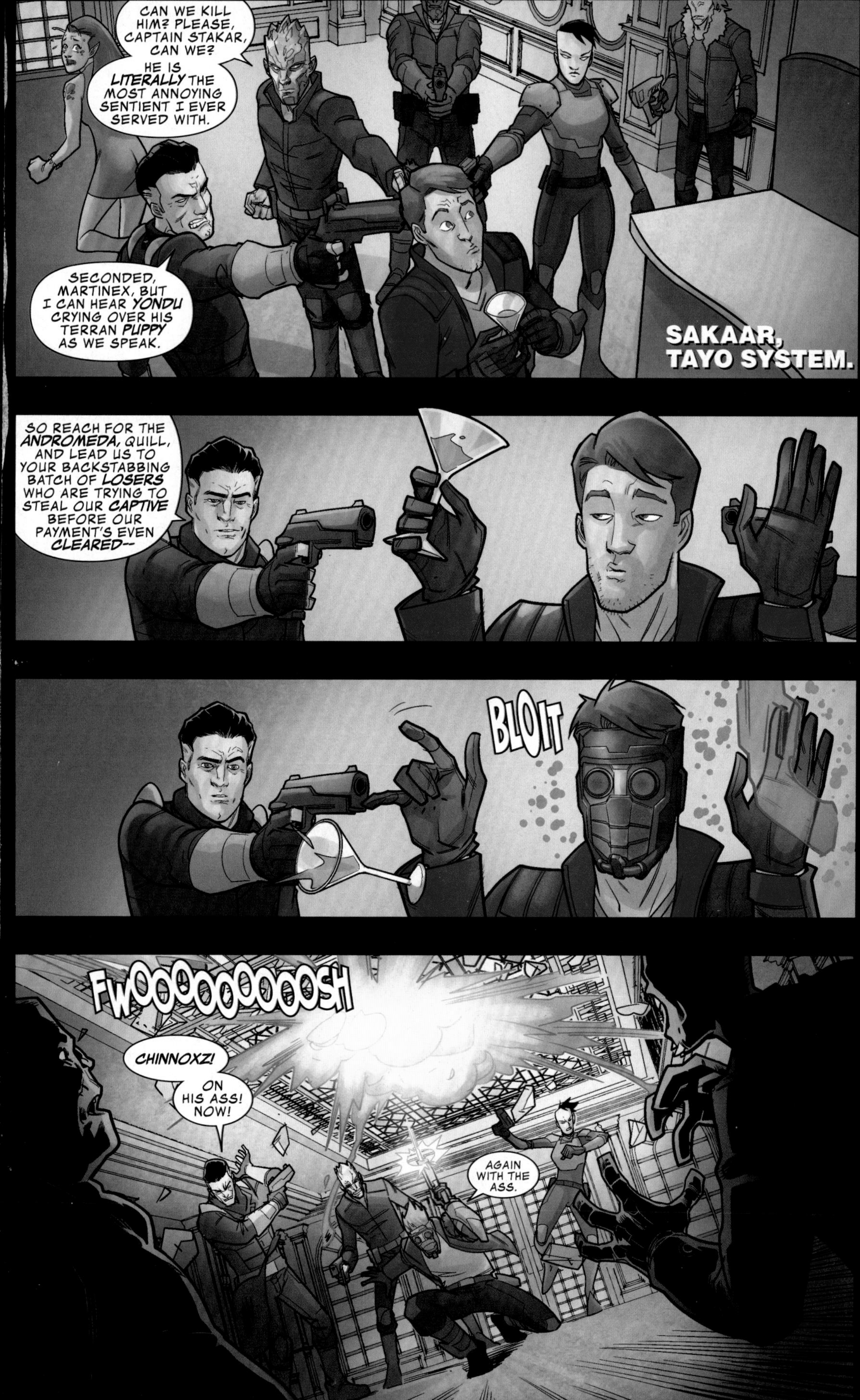
CAN WE KILL HIM? PLEASE, CAPTAIN STAKAR, CAN WE?
HE IS LITERALLY THE MOST ANNOYING SENTIENT I EVER SERVED WITH.
SECONDED, MARTINEX, BUT I CAN HEAR YONDU CRYING OVER HIS TERRAN PUPPY AS WE SPEAK.
SAKAAR, TAYO SYSTEM.
SO REACH FOR THE ANDROMEDA, QUILL, AND LEAD US TO YOUR BACKSTABBING BATCH OF LOSERS WHO ARE TRYING TO STEAL OUR CAPTIVE BEFORE OUR PAYMENT'S EVEN CLEARED--
BLOIT
FWOOOOOOOOOSH
CHINNOXZ!
ON HIS ASS! NOW!
AGAIN WITH THE ASS.

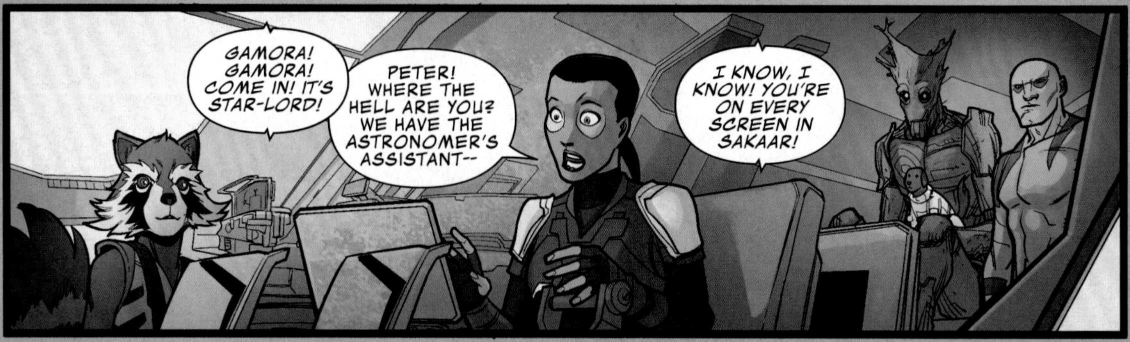
GAMORA! GAMORA! COME IN! IT'S STAR-LORD!
PETER! WHERE THE HELL ARE YOU? WE HAVE THE ASTRONOMER'S ASSISTANT--
I KNOW, I KNOW! YOU'RE ON EVERY SCREEN IN SAKAAR!

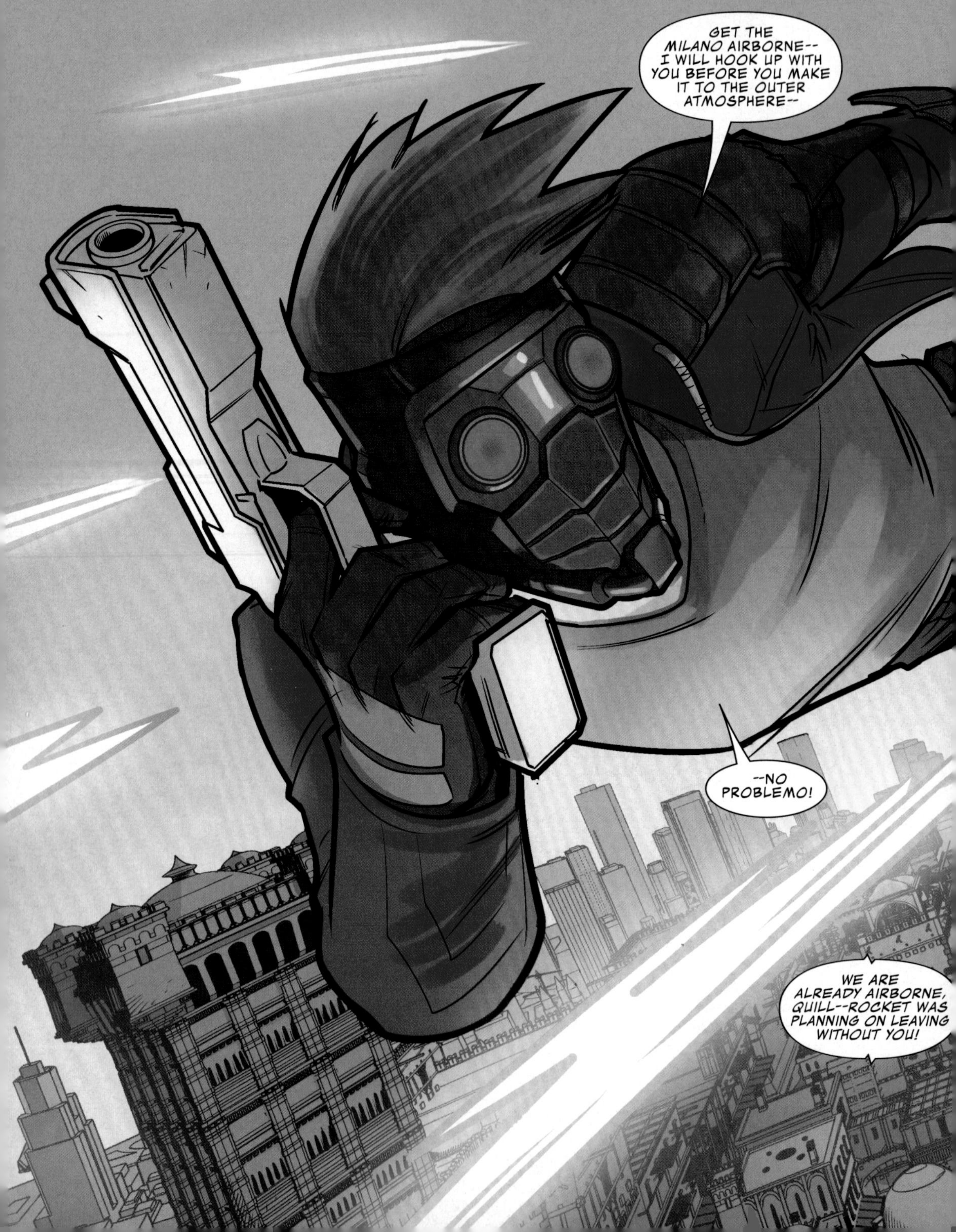
GET THE MILANO AIRBORNE-- I WILL HOOK UP WITH YOU BEFORE YOU MAKE IT TO THE OUTER ATMOSPHERE--
--NO PROBLEMO!
WE ARE ALREADY AIRBORNE, QUILL--ROCKET WAS PLANNING ON LEAVING WITHOUT YOU!

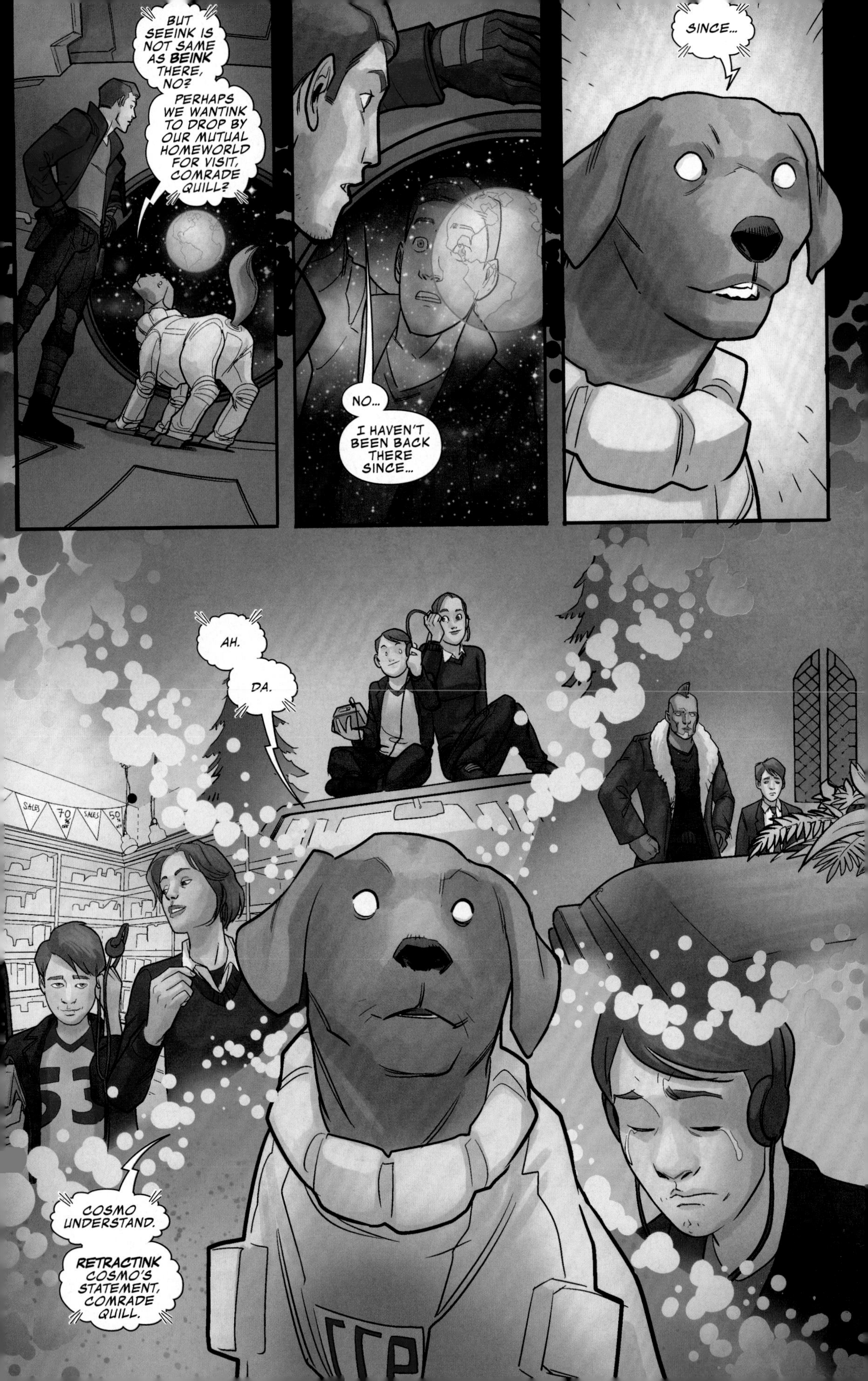
BUT SEEINK IS NOT SAME AS BEINK THERE, NO?
PERHAPS WE WANTINK TO DROP BY OUR MUTUAL HOMEWORLD FOR VISIT, COMRADE QUILL?
NO...
I HAVEN'T BEEN BACK THERE SINCE...
SINCE...
AH.
DA.
SALES
70% OFF
SALES
50%
COSMO UNDERSTAND.
RETRACTINK COSMO'S STATEMENT, COMRADE QUILL.

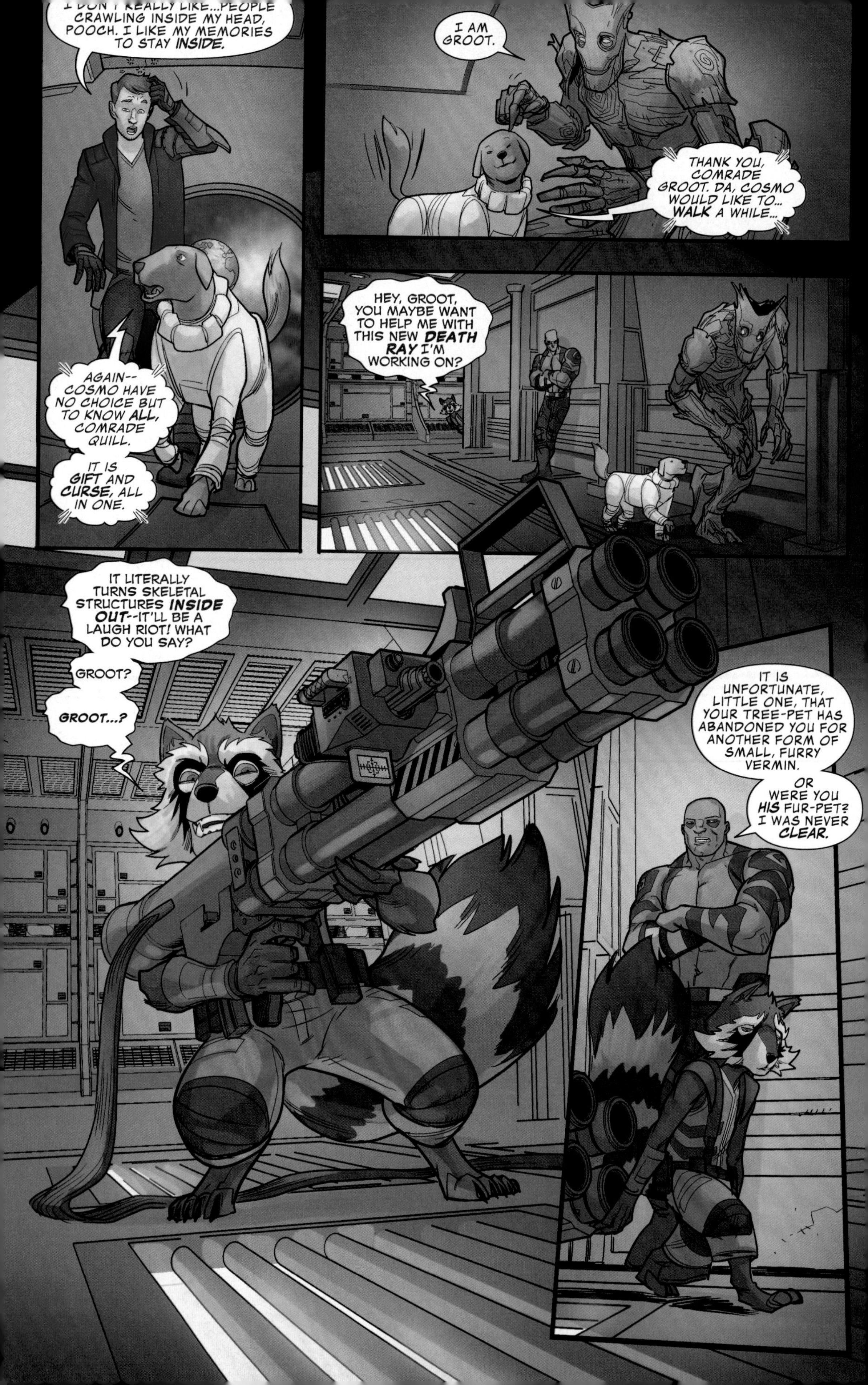
I DON'T REALLY LIKE...PEOPLE CRAWLING INSIDE MY HEAD, POOCH. I LIKE MY MEMORIES TO STAY INSIDE.
AGAIN-- COSMO HAVE NO CHOICE BUT TO KNOW ALL, COMRADE QUILL.
IT IS GIFT AND CURSE, ALL IN ONE.
I AM GROOT.
THANK YOU, COMRADE GROOT. DA, COSMO WOULD LIKE TO... WALK A WHILE...
HEY, GROOT, YOU MAYBE WANT TO HELP ME WITH THIS NEW DEATH RAY I'M WORKING ON?
IT LITERALLY TURNS SKELETAL STRUCTURES INSIDE OUT--IT'LL BE A LAUGH RIOT! WHAT DO YOU SAY?
GROOT?
GROOT...?
IT IS UNFORTUNATE, LITTLE ONE, THAT YOUR TREE-PET HAS ABANDONED YOU FOR ANOTHER FORM OF SMALL, FURRY VERMIN.
OR WERE YOU HIS FUR-PET? I WAS NEVER CLEAR.

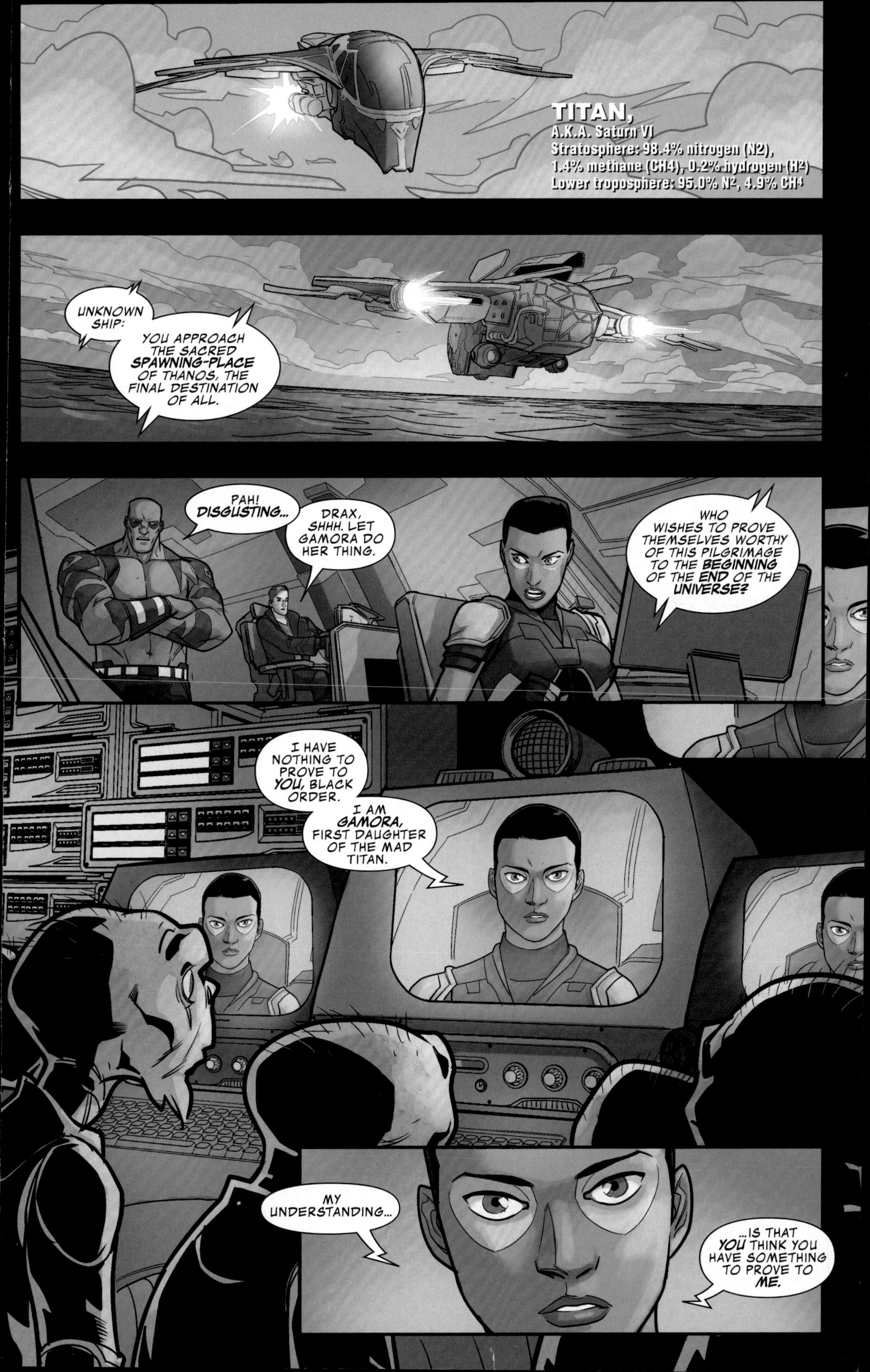
TITAN,
A.K.A. Saturn VI
Stratosphere: 98.4% nitrogen (N2), 1.4% methane (CH4), 0.2% hydrogen (H2)
Lower troposphere: 95.0% N2, 4.9% CH4
UNKNOWN SHIP:
YOU APPROACH THE SACRED SPAWNING-PLACE OF THANOS, THE FINAL DESTINATION OF ALL.
PAH! DISGUSTING...
DRAX, SHHH. LET GAMORA DO HER THING.
WHO WISHES TO PROVE THEMSELVES WORTHY OF THIS PILGRIMAGE TO THE BEGINNING OF THE END OF THE UNIVERSE?
I HAVE NOTHING TO PROVE TO YOU, BLACK ORDER.
I AM GAMORA, FIRST DAUGHTER OF THE MAD TITAN.
MY UNDERSTANDING...
...IS THAT YOU THINK YOU HAVE SOMETHING TO PROVE TO ME.

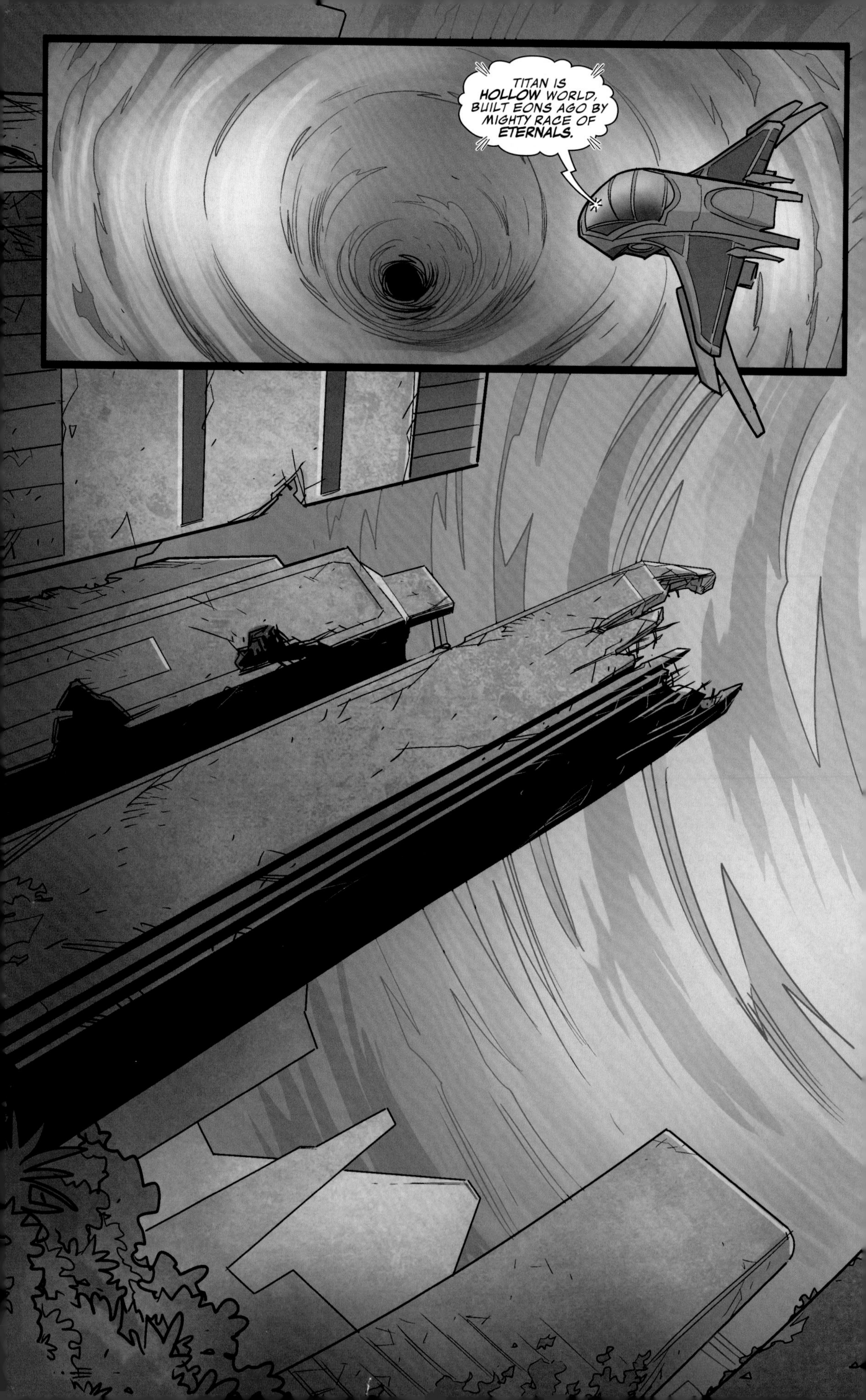
TITAN IS HOLLOW WORLD, BUILT EONS AGO BY MIGHTY RACE OF ETERNALS.

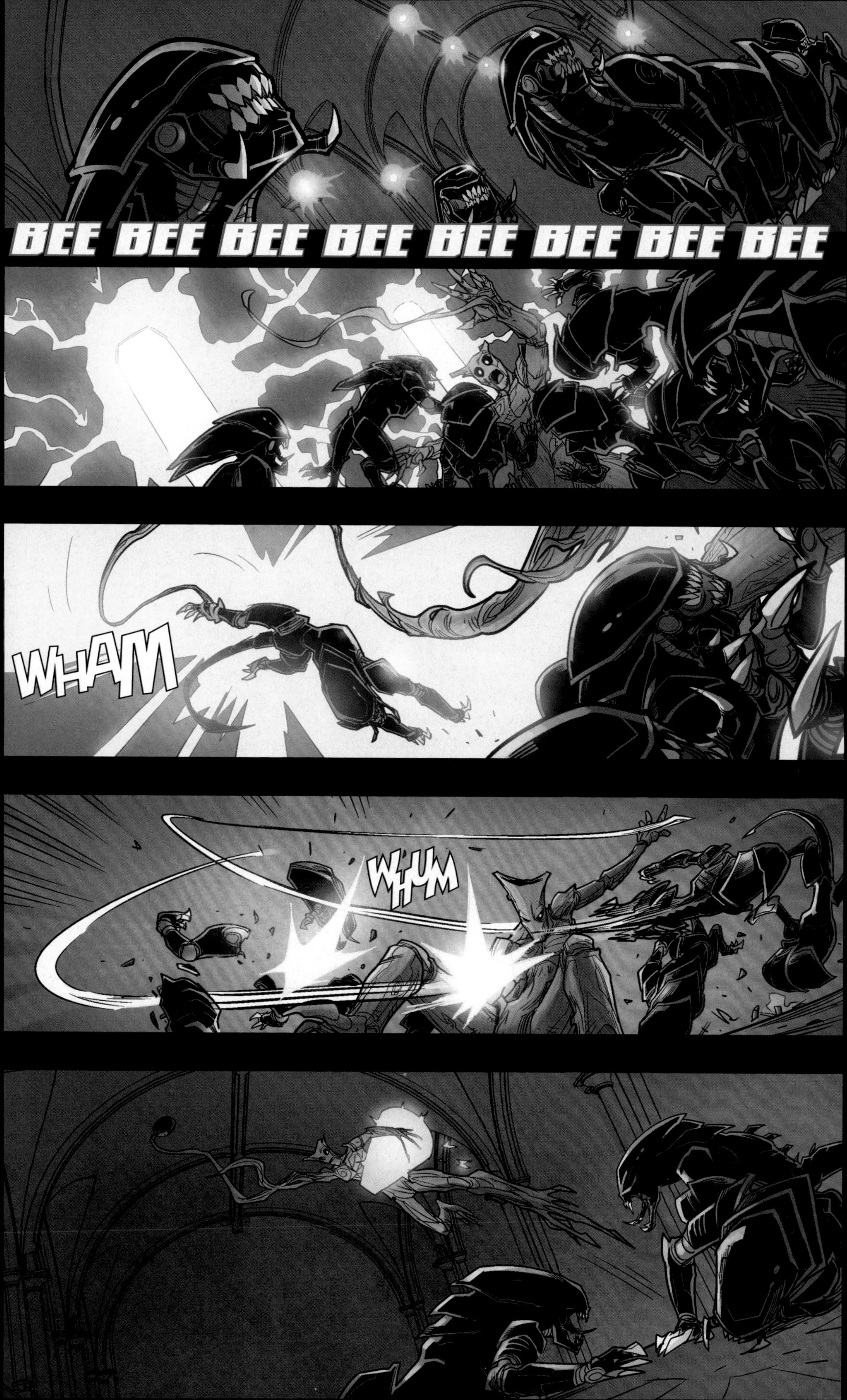
BEE BEE BEE BEE BEE BEE BEE BEE
WHAM
WHUM

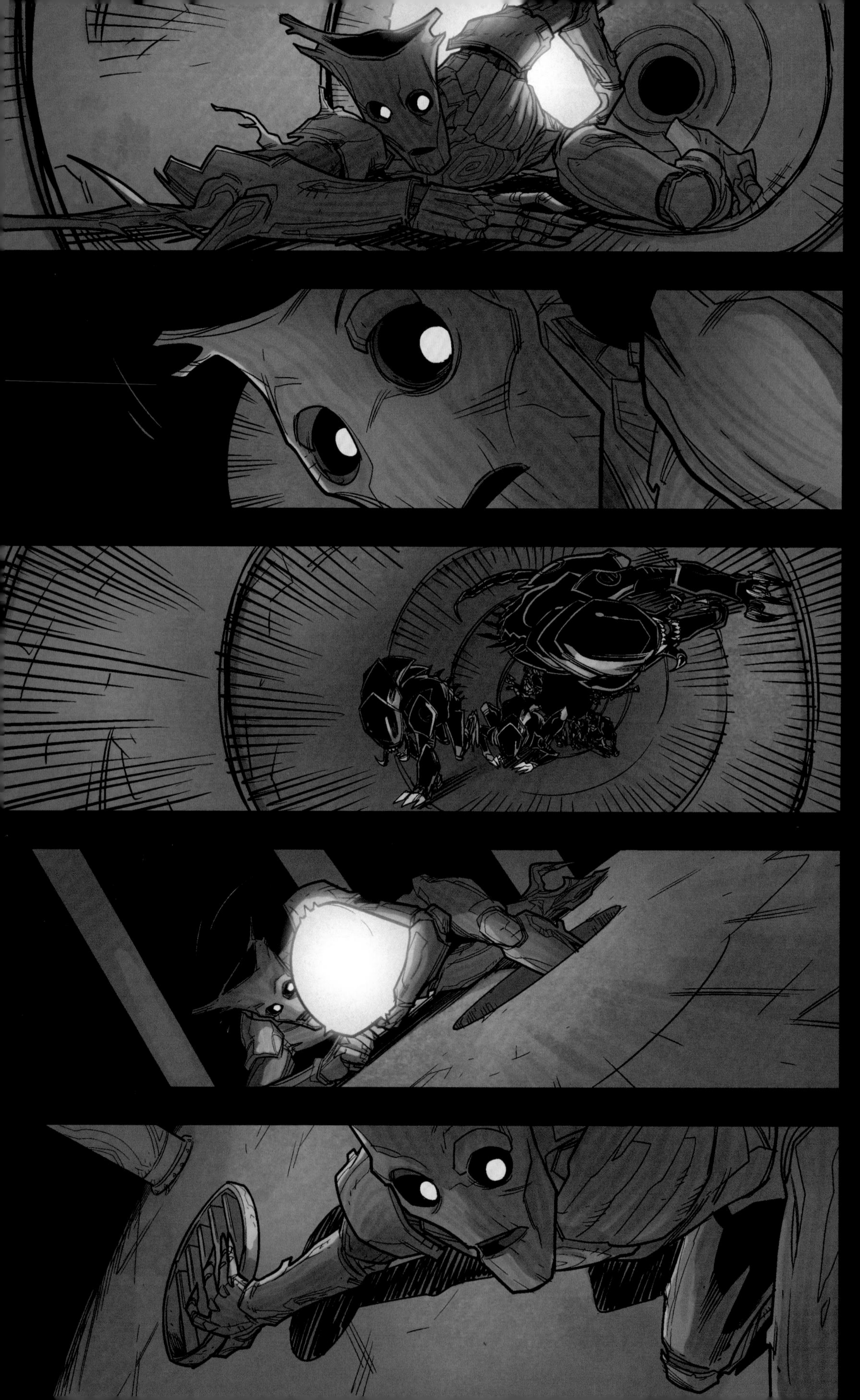

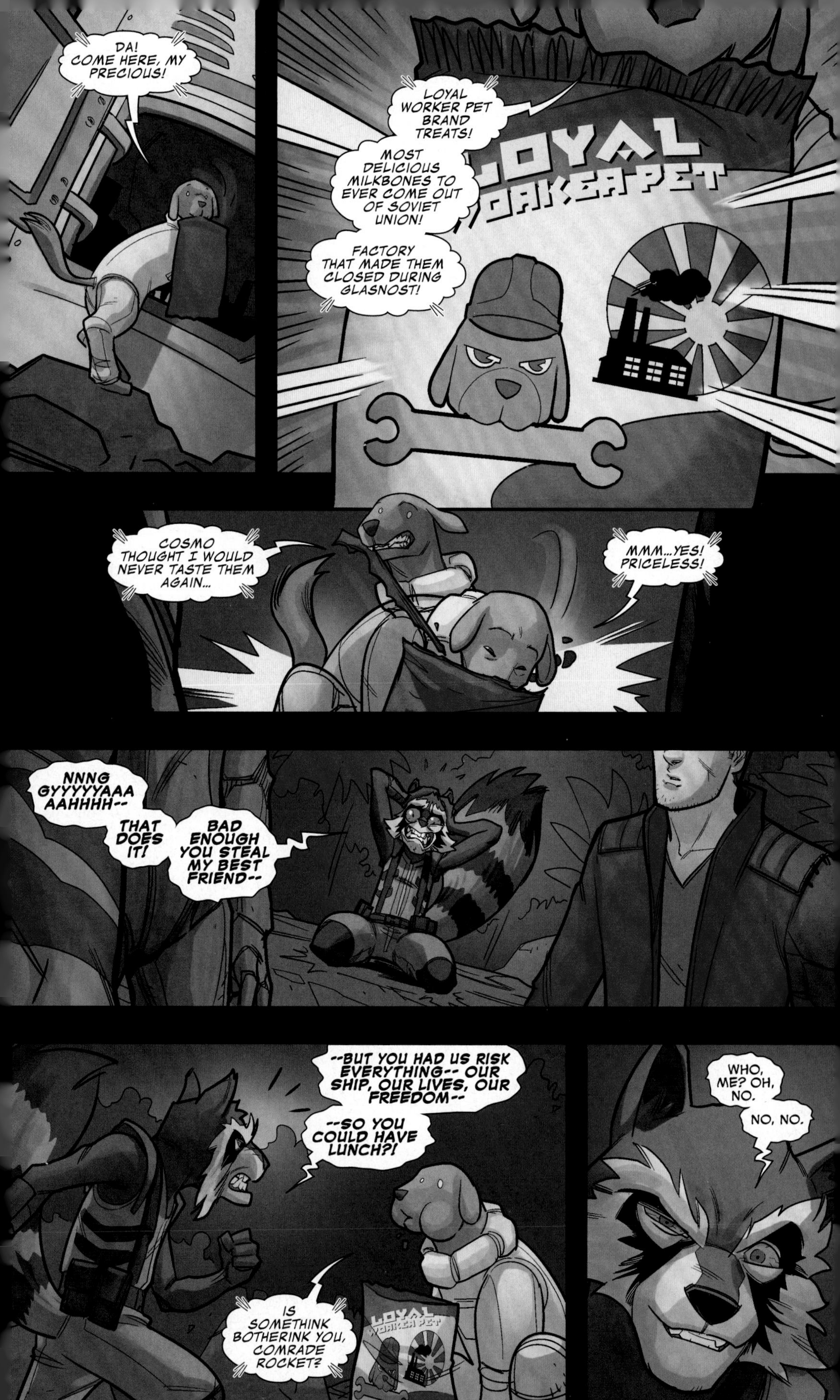
DA! COME HERE, MY PRECIOUS!
LOYAL WORKER PET BRAND TREATS!
MOST DELICIOUS MILKBONES TO EVER COME OUT OF SOVIET UNION!
FACTORY THAT MADE THEM CLOSED DURING GLASNOST!
LOYAL WORKER PET
COSMO THOUGHT I WOULD NEVER TASTE THEM AGAIN...
MMM...YES! PRICELESS!
NNNG GYYYYYAAA AAHHHH--
THAT DOES IT!
BAD ENOUGH YOU STEAL MY BEST FRIEND--
--BUT YOU HAD US RISK EVERYTHING-- OUR SHIP, OUR LIVES, OUR FREEDOM--
--SO YOU COULD HAVE LUNCH?!
IS SOMETHINK BOTHERINK YOU, COMRADE ROCKET?
LOYAL WORKER PET
WHO, ME? OH, NO.
NO, NO.

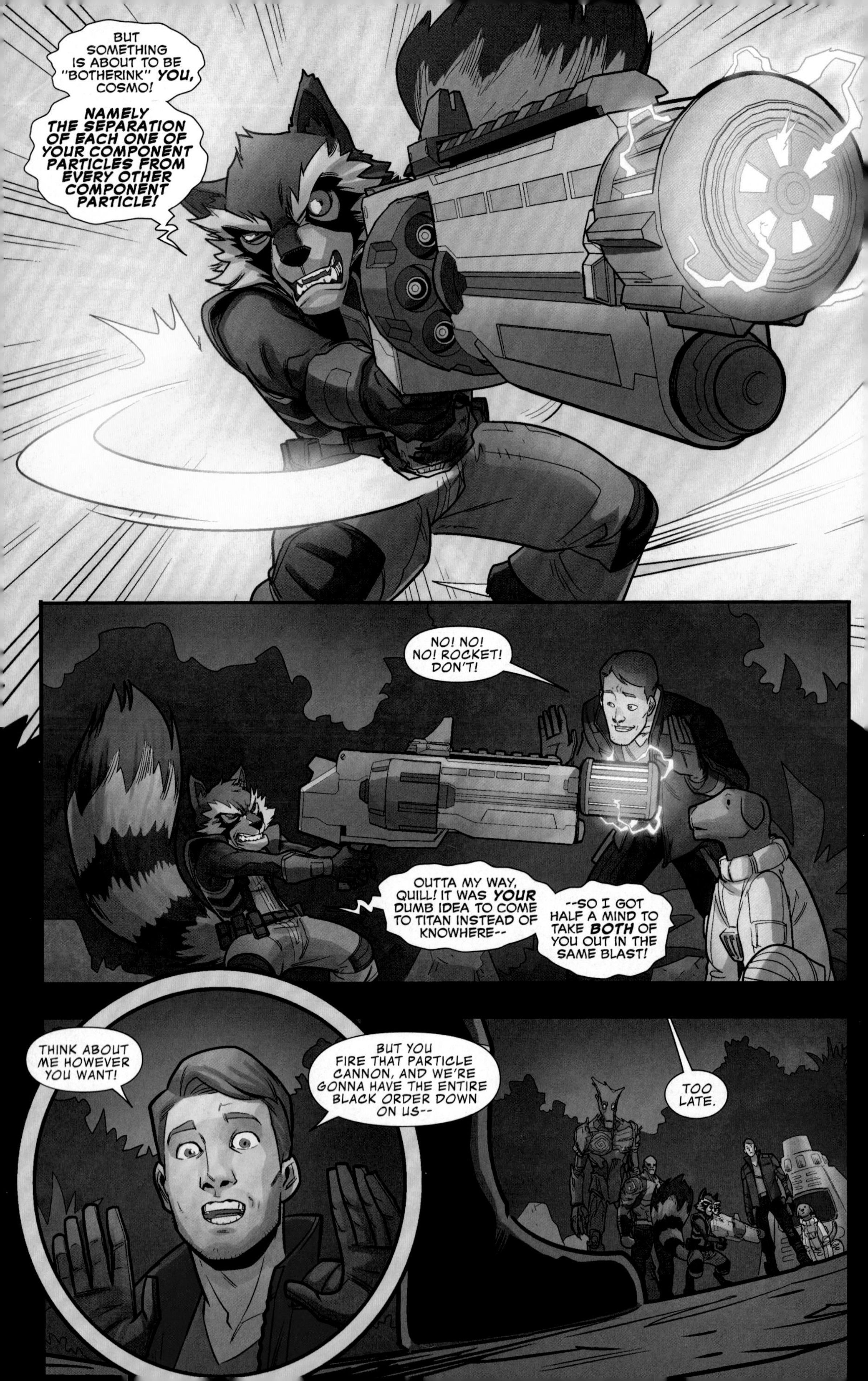

BUT SOMETHING IS ABOUT TO BE "BOTHERINK" ***YOU,*** COSMO!
NAMELY THE SEPARATION OF EACH ONE OF YOUR COMPONENT PARTICLES FROM EVERY OTHER COMPONENT PARTICLE!
NO! NO! NO! ROCKET! DON'T!
OUTTA MY WAY, QUILL! IT WAS ***YOUR*** DUMB IDEA TO COME TO TITAN INSTEAD OF KNOWHERE--
--SO I GOT HALF A MIND TO TAKE ***BOTH*** OF YOU OUT IN THE SAME BLAST!
THINK ABOUT ME HOWEVER YOU WANT!
BUT YOU FIRE THAT PARTICLE CANNON, AND WE'RE GONNA HAVE THE ENTIRE BLACK ORDER DOWN ON US--
TOO LATE.

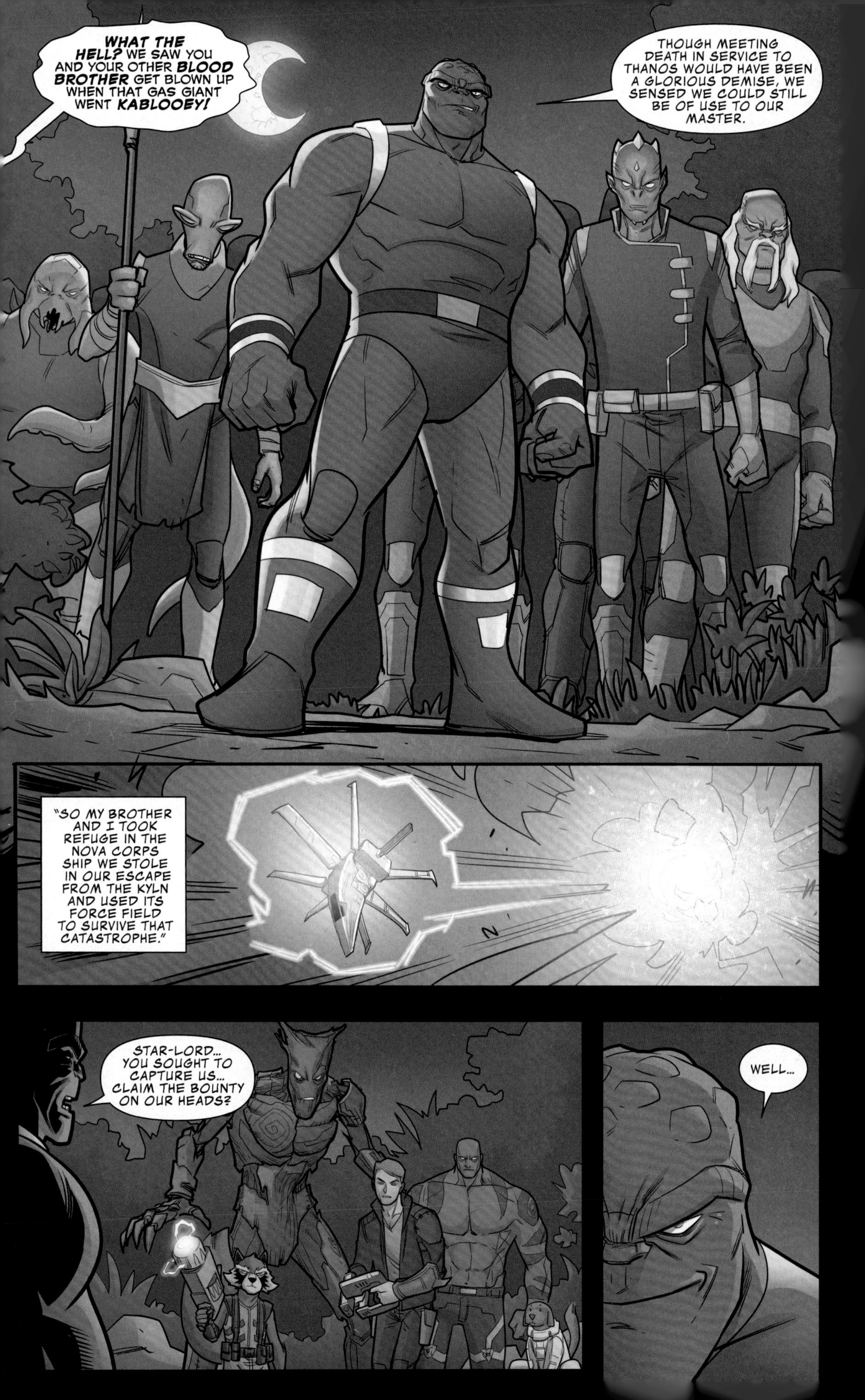
WHAT THE HELL? WE SAW YOU AND YOUR OTHER BLOOD BROTHER GET BLOWN UP WHEN THAT GAS GIANT WENT KABLOOEY!
THOUGH MEETING DEATH IN SERVICE TO THANOS WOULD HAVE BEEN A GLORIOUS DEMISE, WE SENSED WE COULD STILL BE OF USE TO OUR MASTER.
"SO MY BROTHER AND I TOOK REFUGE IN THE NOVA CORPS SHIP WE STOLE IN OUR ESCAPE FROM THE KYLN AND USED ITS FORCE FIELD TO SURVIVE THAT CATASTROPHE."
STAR-LORD... YOU SOUGHT TO CAPTURE US... CLAIM THE BOUNTY ON OUR HEADS?
WELL...

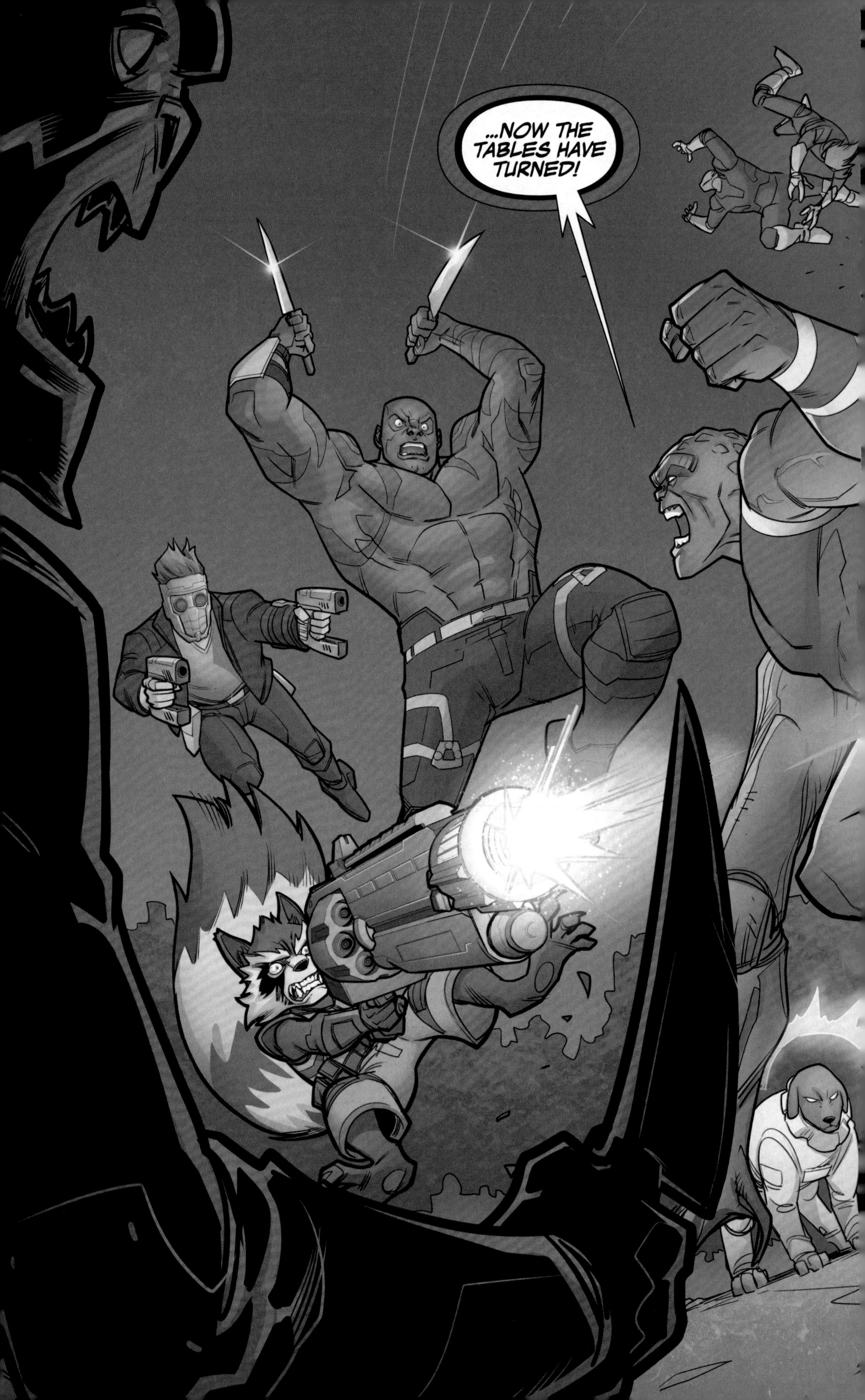
...NOW THE TABLES HAVE TURNED!

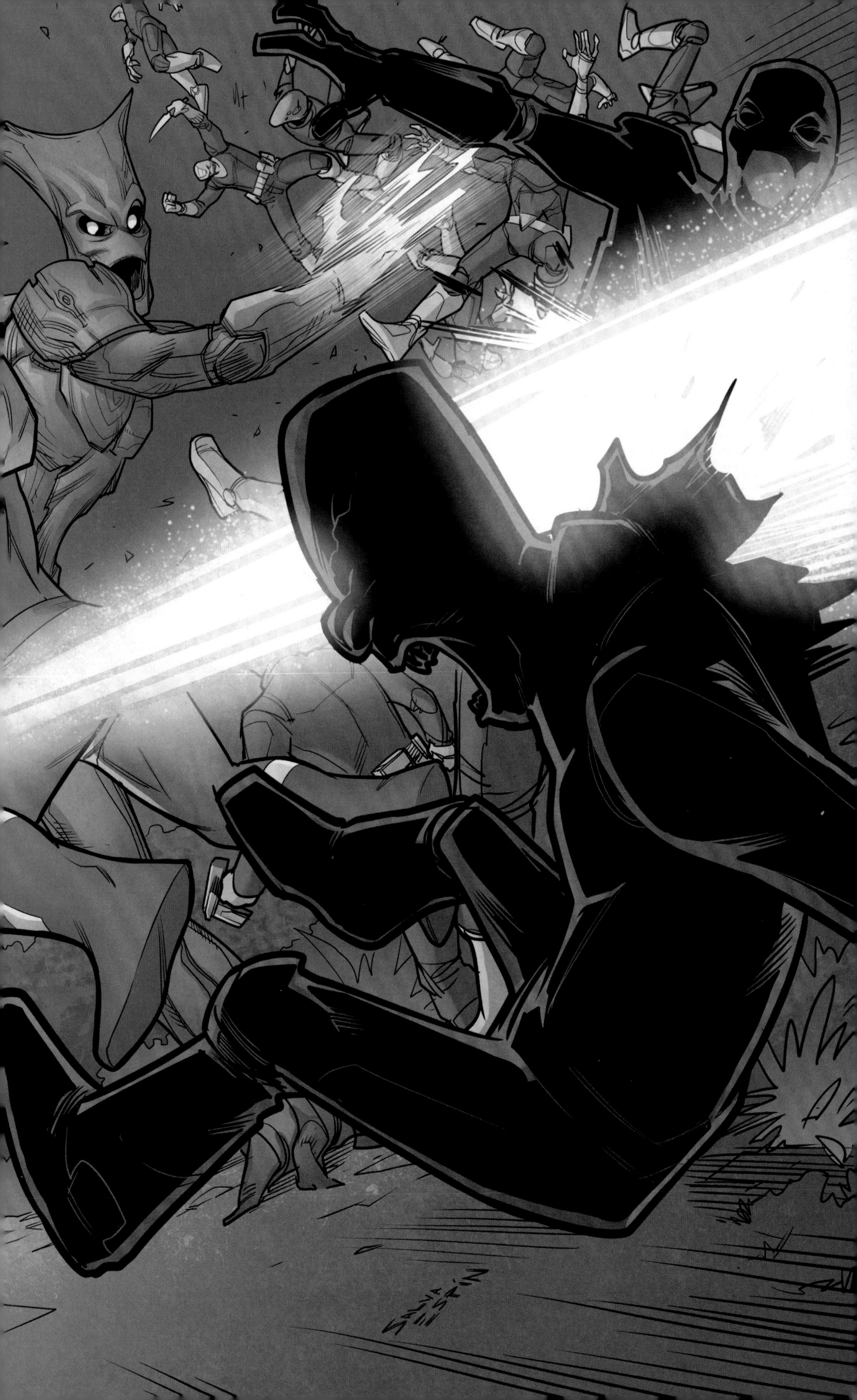
SALVA ESPIN

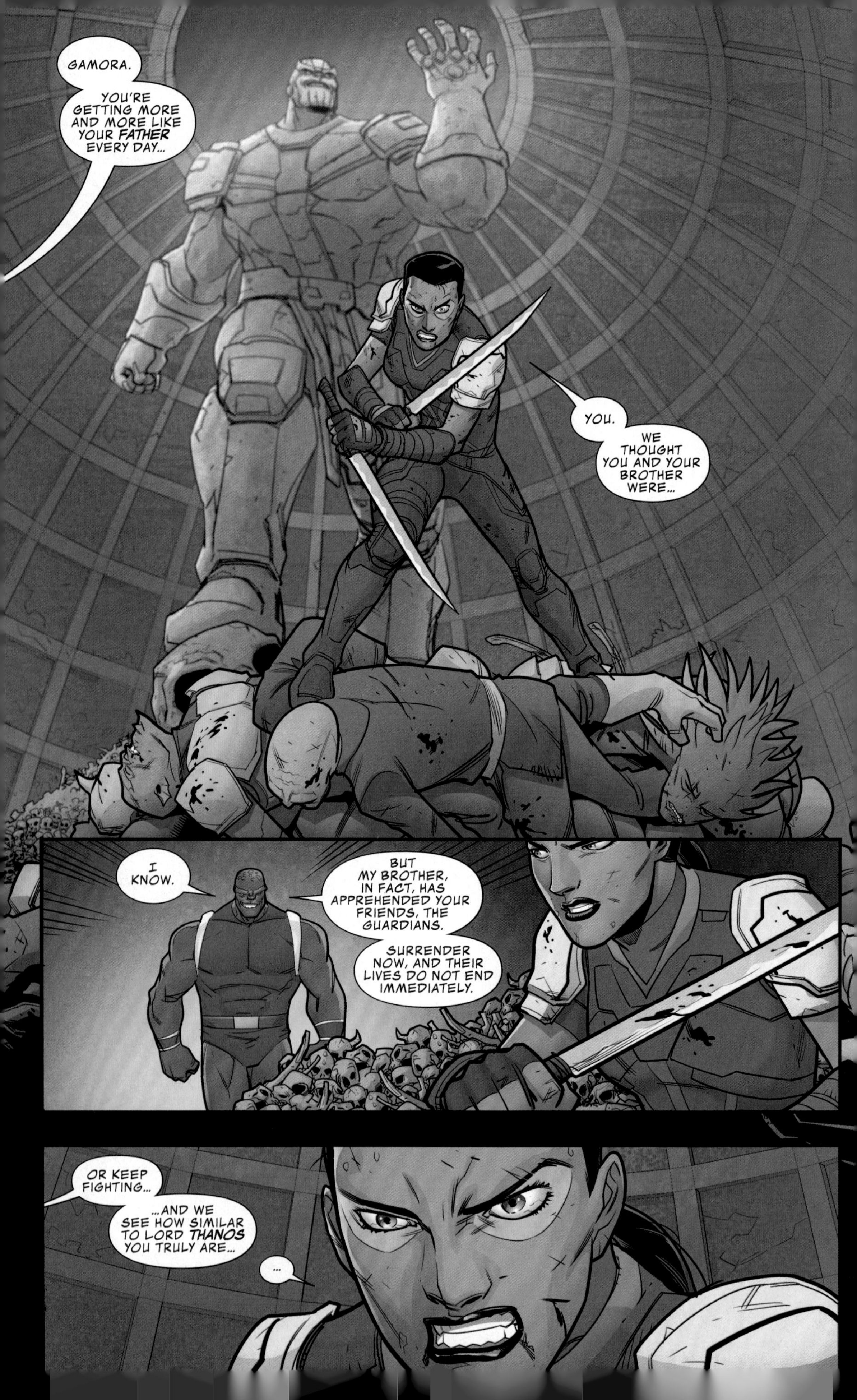
GAMORA.
YOU'RE GETTING MORE AND MORE LIKE YOUR FATHER EVERY DAY...
YOU.
WE THOUGHT YOU AND YOUR BROTHER WERE...
I KNOW.
BUT MY BROTHER, IN FACT, HAS APPREHENDED YOUR FRIENDS, THE GUARDIANS.
SURRENDER NOW, AND THEIR LIVES DO NOT END IMMEDIATELY.
OR KEEP FIGHTING...
...AND WE SEE HOW SIMILAR TO LORD THANOS YOU TRULY ARE...
...

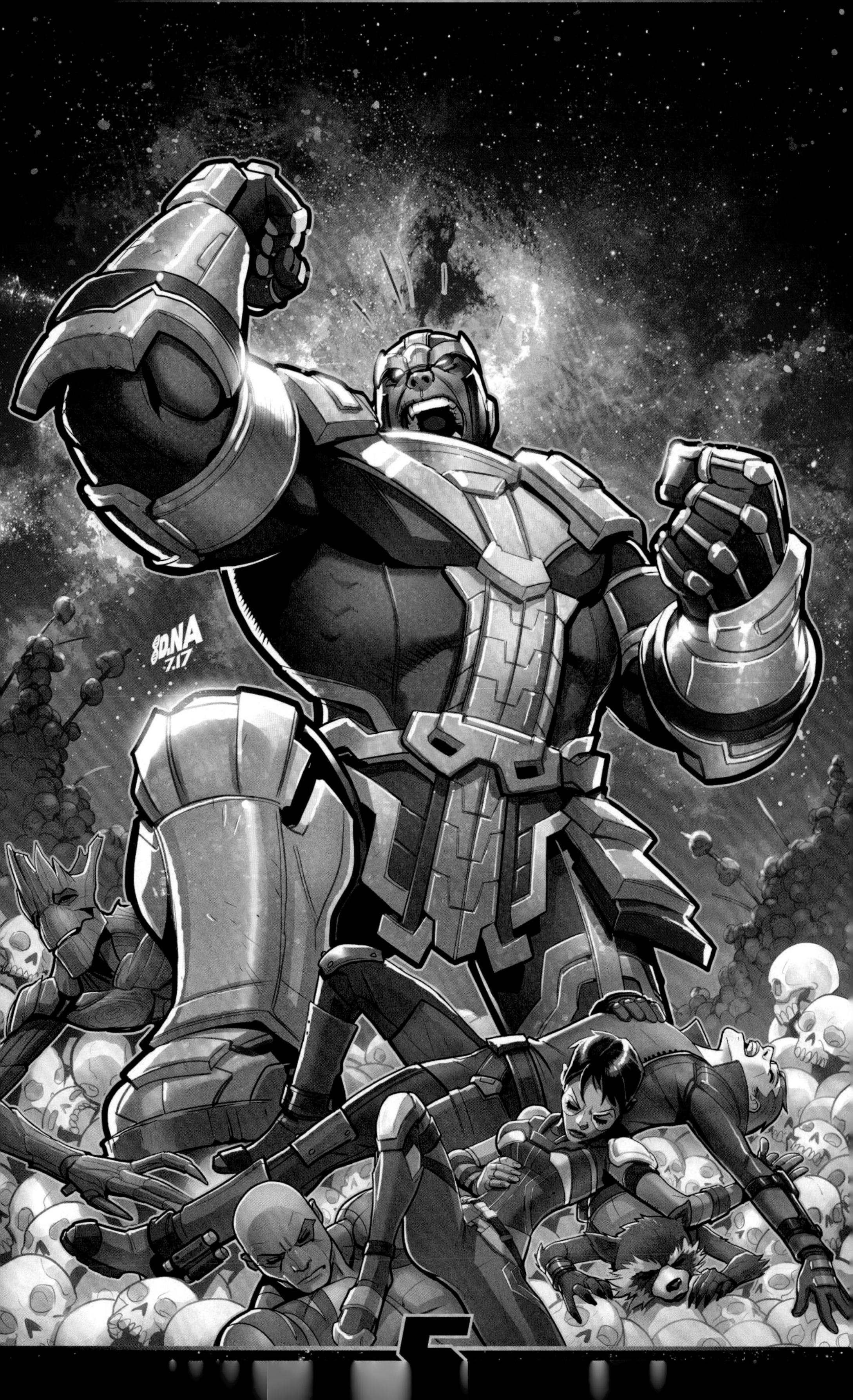
D.NA
7.17

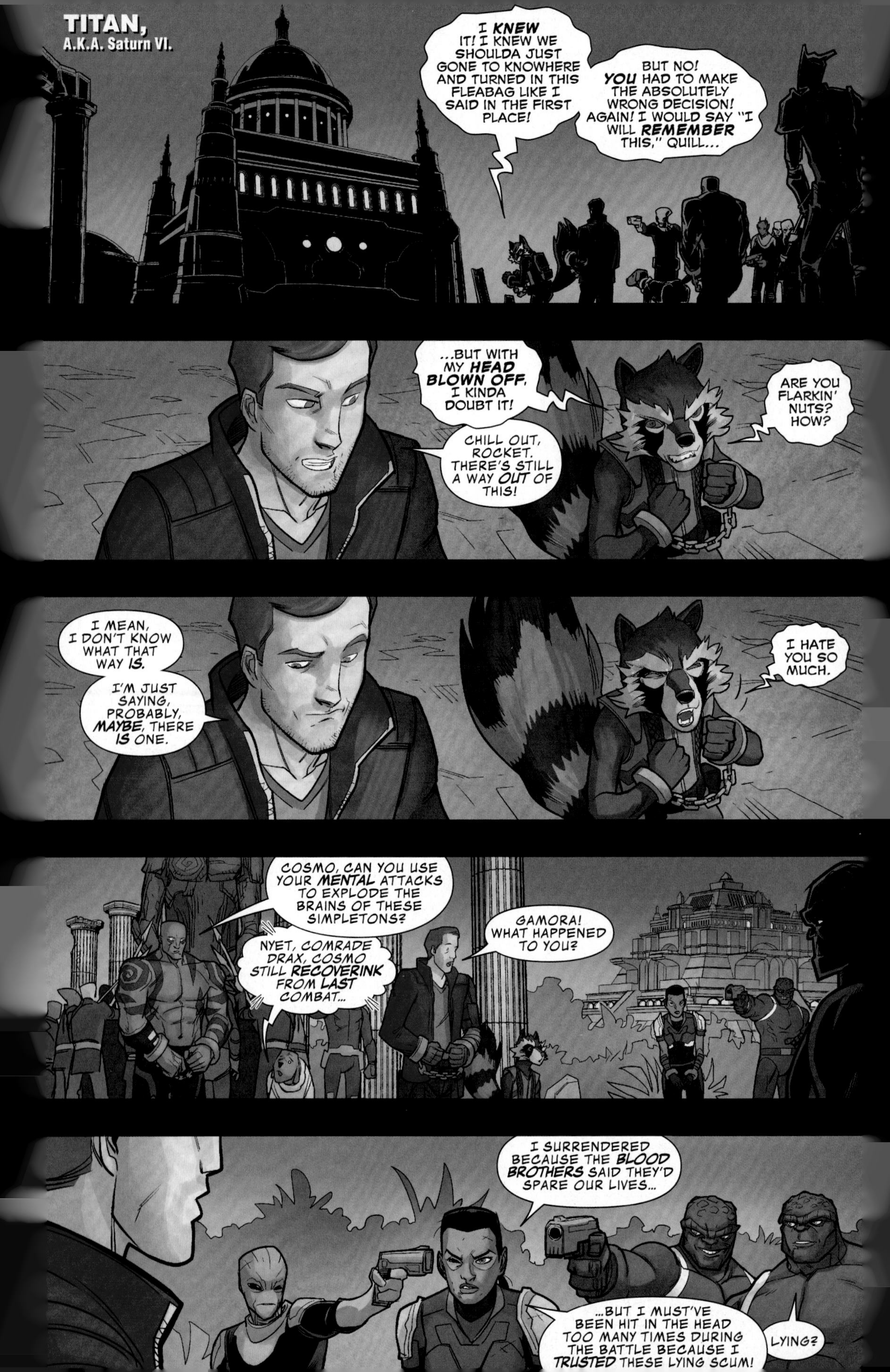
TITAN,
A.K.A. Saturn VI.
I KNEW IT! I KNEW WE SHOULDA JUST GONE TO KNOWHERE AND TURNED IN THIS FLEABAG LIKE I SAID IN THE FIRST PLACE!
BUT NO! YOU HAD TO MAKE THE ABSOLUTELY WRONG DECISION! AGAIN! I WOULD SAY "I WILL REMEMBER THIS," QUILL...
...BUT WITH MY HEAD BLOWN OFF, I KINDA DOUBT IT!
CHILL OUT, ROCKET. THERE'S STILL A WAY OUT OF THIS!
ARE YOU FLARKIN' NUTS? HOW?
I MEAN, I DON'T KNOW WHAT THAT WAY IS.
I'M JUST SAYING, PROBABLY, MAYBE, THERE IS ONE.
I HATE YOU SO MUCH.
COSMO, CAN YOU USE YOUR MENTAL ATTACKS TO EXPLODE THE BRAINS OF THESE SIMPLETONS?
NYET, COMRADE DRAX, COSMO STILL RECOVERINK FROM LAST COMBAT...
GAMORA! WHAT HAPPENED TO YOU?
I SURRENDERED BECAUSE THE BLOOD BROTHERS SAID THEY'D SPARE OUR LIVES...
...BUT I MUST'VE BEEN HIT IN THE HEAD TOO MANY TIMES DURING THE BATTLE BECAUSE I TRUSTED THESE LYING SCUM!
LYING?

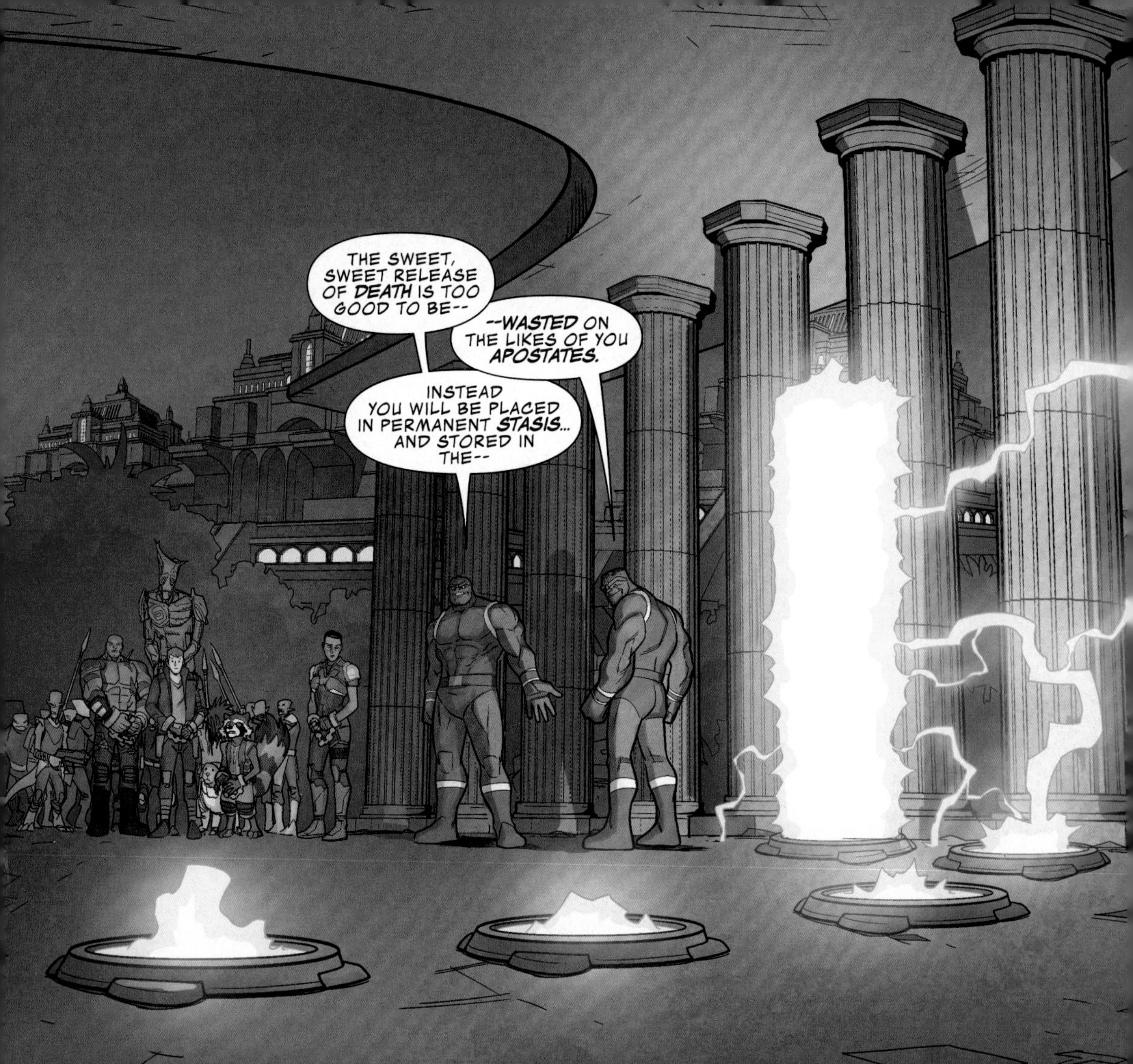
THE SWEET, SWEET RELEASE OF DEATH IS TOO GOOD TO BE--
--WASTED ON THE LIKES OF YOU APOSTATES.
INSTEAD YOU WILL BE PLACED IN PERMANENT STASIS... AND STORED IN THE--
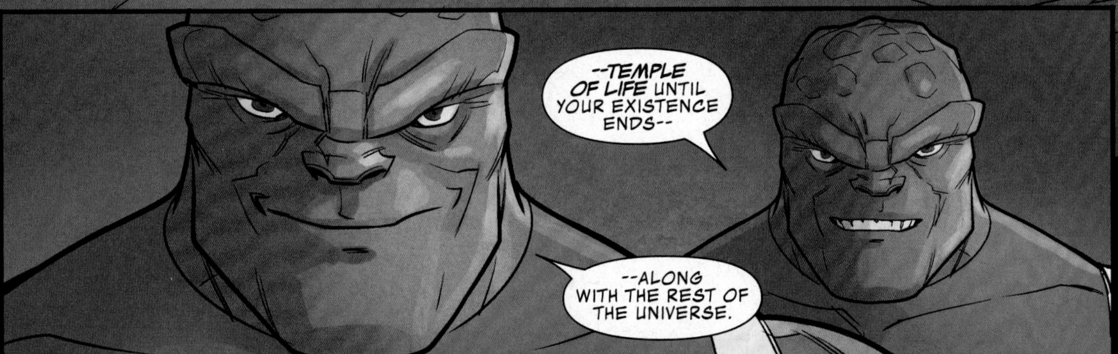
--TEMPLE OF LIFE UNTIL YOUR EXISTENCE ENDS--
--ALONG WITH THE REST OF THE UNIVERSE.
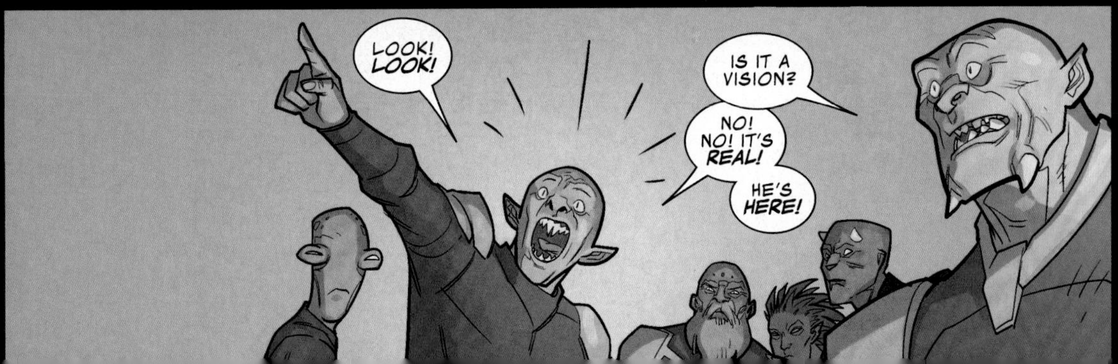
LOOK! LOOK!
IS IT A VISION?
NO! NO! IT'S REAL!
HE'S HERE!

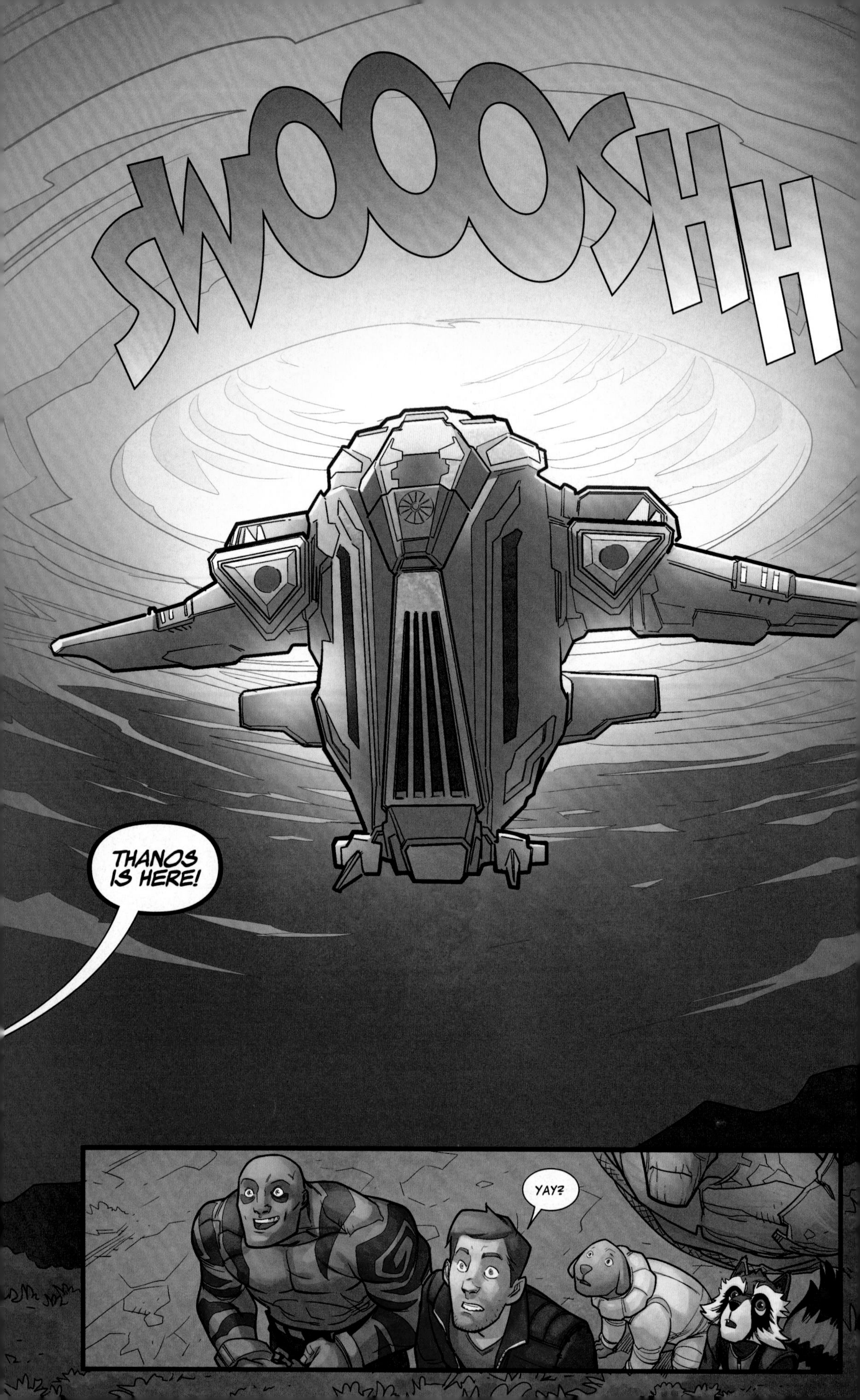
SWOOOSHH
THANOS IS HERE!
YAY?

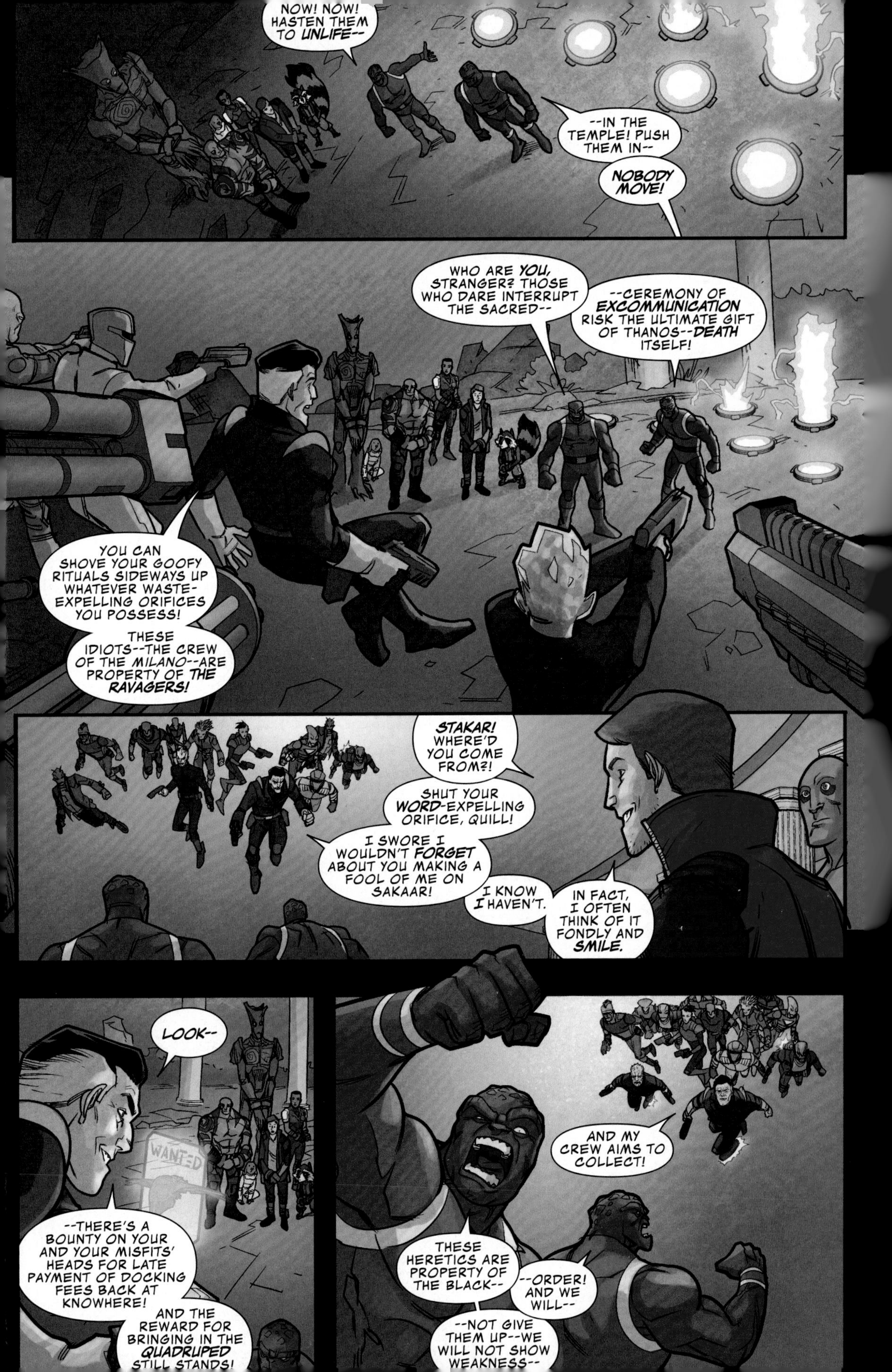
NOW! NOW! HASTEN THEM TO UNLIFE--
--IN THE TEMPLE! PUSH THEM IN--
NOBODY MOVE!
WHO ARE YOU, STRANGER? THOSE WHO DARE INTERRUPT THE SACRED--
--CEREMONY OF EXCOMMUNICATION RISK THE ULTIMATE GIFT OF THANOS--DEATH ITSELF!
YOU CAN SHOVE YOUR GOOFY RITUALS SIDEWAYS UP WHATEVER WASTE-EXPELLING ORIFICES YOU POSSESS!
THESE IDIOTS--THE CREW OF THE MILANO--ARE PROPERTY OF THE RAVAGERS!
STAKAR! WHERE'D YOU COME FROM?!
SHUT YOUR WORD-EXPELLING ORIFICE, QUILL!
I SWORE I WOULDN'T FORGET ABOUT YOU MAKING A FOOL OF ME ON SAKAAR!
I KNOW I HAVEN'T.
IN FACT, I OFTEN THINK OF IT FONDLY AND SMILE.
LOOK--
WANTED
--THERE'S A BOUNTY ON YOUR AND YOUR MISFITS' HEADS FOR LATE PAYMENT OF DOCKING FEES BACK AT KNOWHERE!
AND THE REWARD FOR BRINGING IN THE QUADRUPED STILL STANDS!
AND MY CREW AIMS TO COLLECT!
THESE HERETICS ARE PROPERTY OF THE BLACK--
--ORDER! AND WE WILL--
--NOT GIVE THEM UP--WE WILL NOT SHOW WEAKNESS--

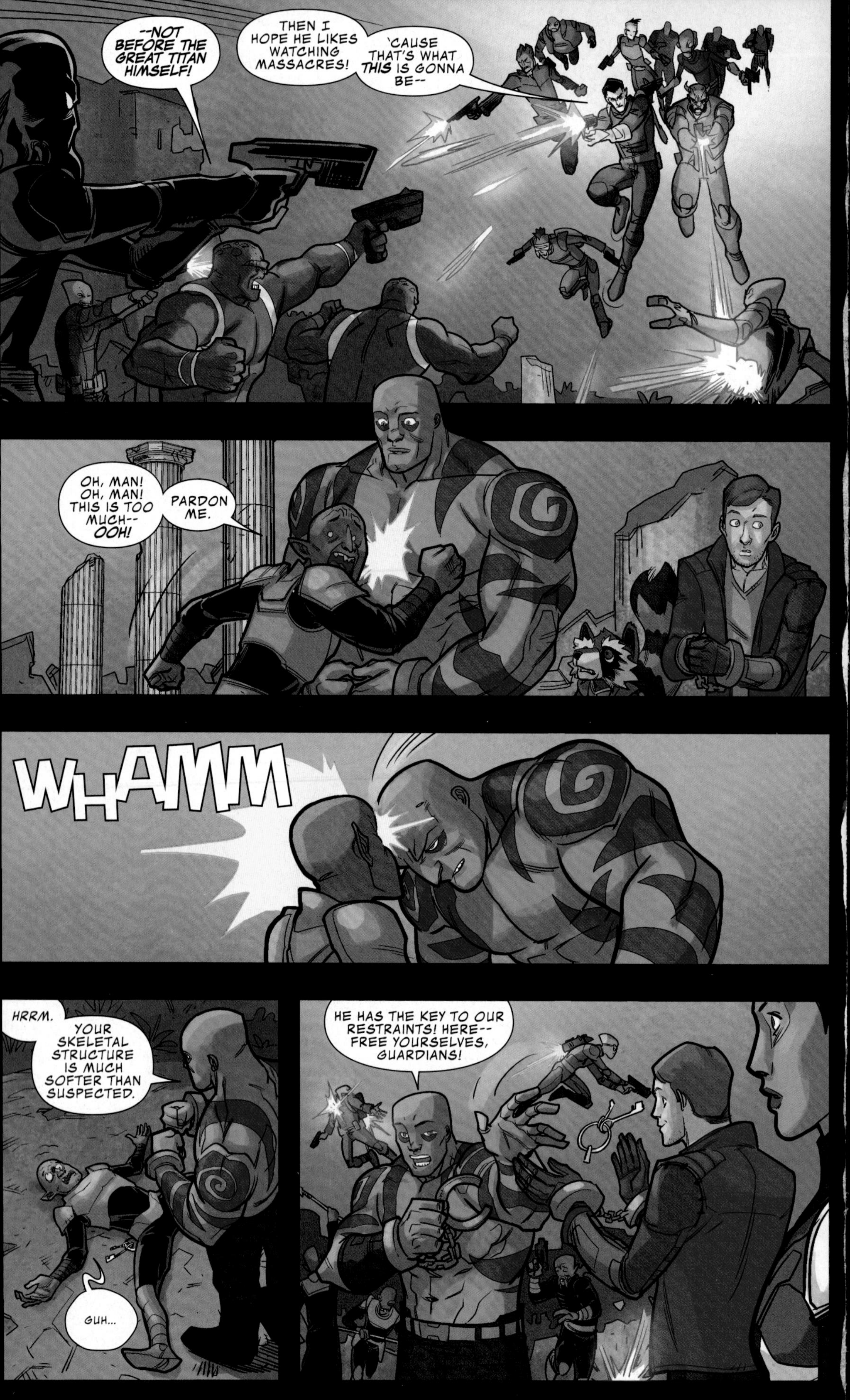

--NOT BEFORE THE GREAT TITAN HIMSELF!
THEN I HOPE HE LIKES WATCHING MASSACRES!
'CAUSE THAT'S WHAT THIS IS GONNA BE--
OH, MAN! OH, MAN! THIS IS TOO MUCH-- OOH!
PARDON ME.
WHAMM
HRRM.
YOUR SKELETAL STRUCTURE IS MUCH SOFTER THAN SUSPECTED.
GUH...
HE HAS THE KEY TO OUR RESTRAINTS! HERE-- FREE YOURSELVES, GUARDIANS!

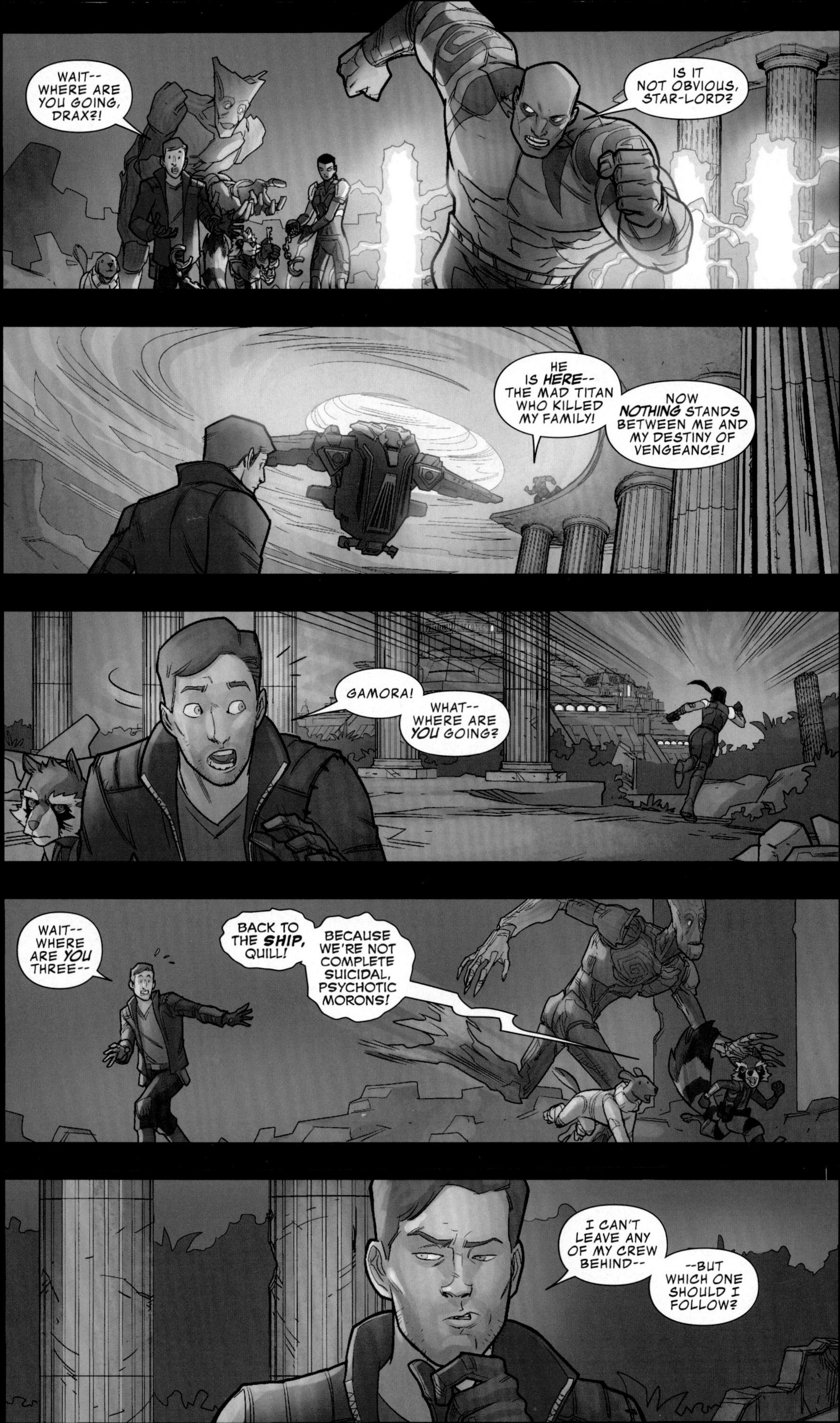
WAIT-- WHERE ARE YOU GOING, DRAX?!
IS IT NOT OBVIOUS, STAR-LORD?
HE IS HERE-- THE MAD TITAN WHO KILLED MY FAMILY!
NOW NOTHING STANDS BETWEEN ME AND MY DESTINY OF VENGEANCE!
GAMORA!
WHAT-- WHERE ARE YOU GOING?
WAIT-- WHERE ARE YOU THREE--
BACK TO THE SHIP, QUILL!
BECAUSE WE'RE NOT COMPLETE SUICIDAL, PSYCHOTIC MORONS!
I CAN'T LEAVE ANY OF MY CREW BEHIND--
--BUT WHICH ONE SHOULD I FOLLOW?

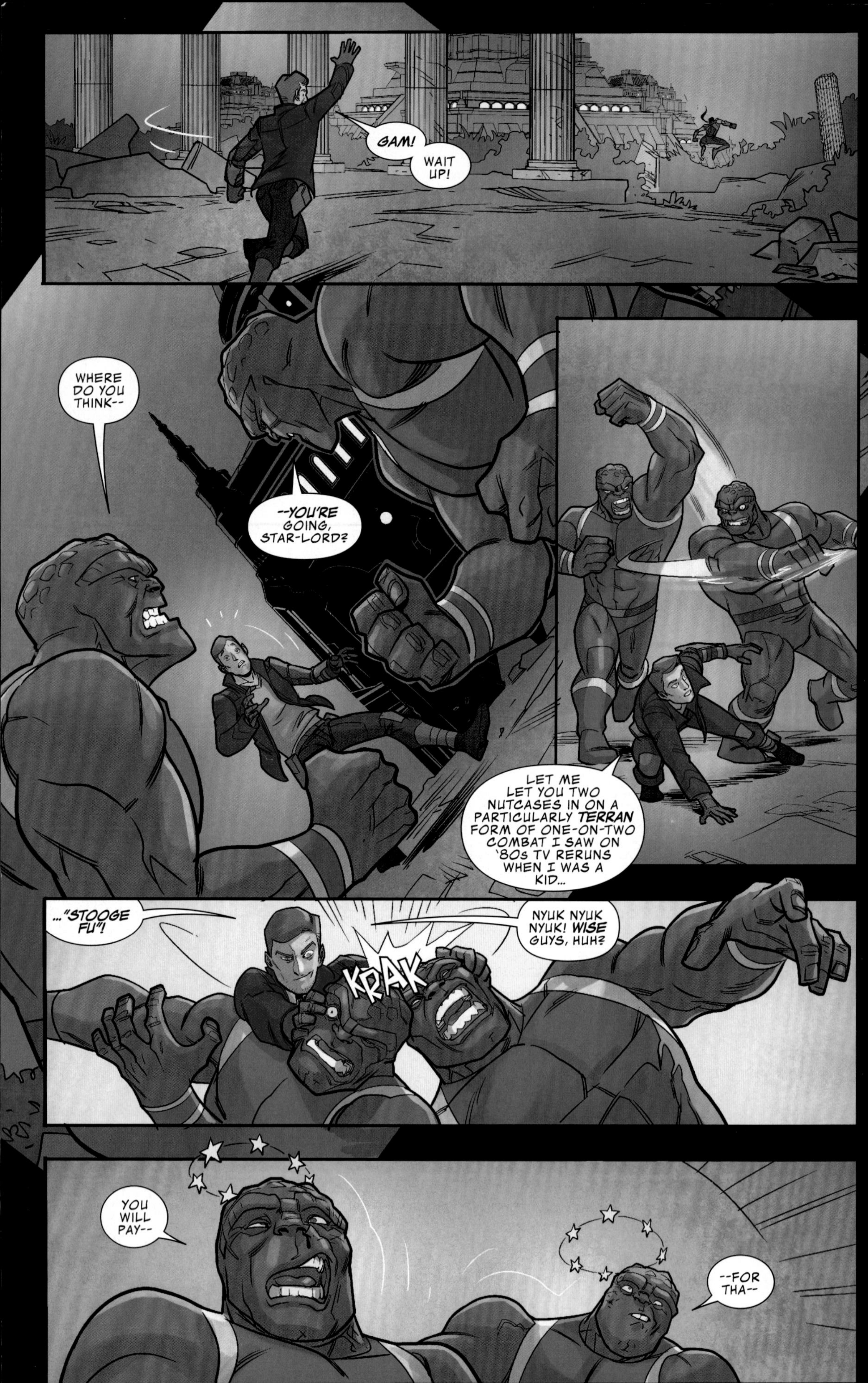

GAM!
WAIT UP!
WHERE DO YOU THINK--
--YOU'RE GOING, STAR-LORD?
LET ME LET YOU TWO NUTCASES IN ON A PARTICULARLY TERRAN FORM OF ONE-ON-TWO COMBAT I SAW ON '80s TV RERUNS WHEN I WAS A KID...
..."STOOGE FU"!
NYUK NYUK NYUK! WISE GUYS, HUH?
KRAK
YOU WILL PAY--
--FOR THA--

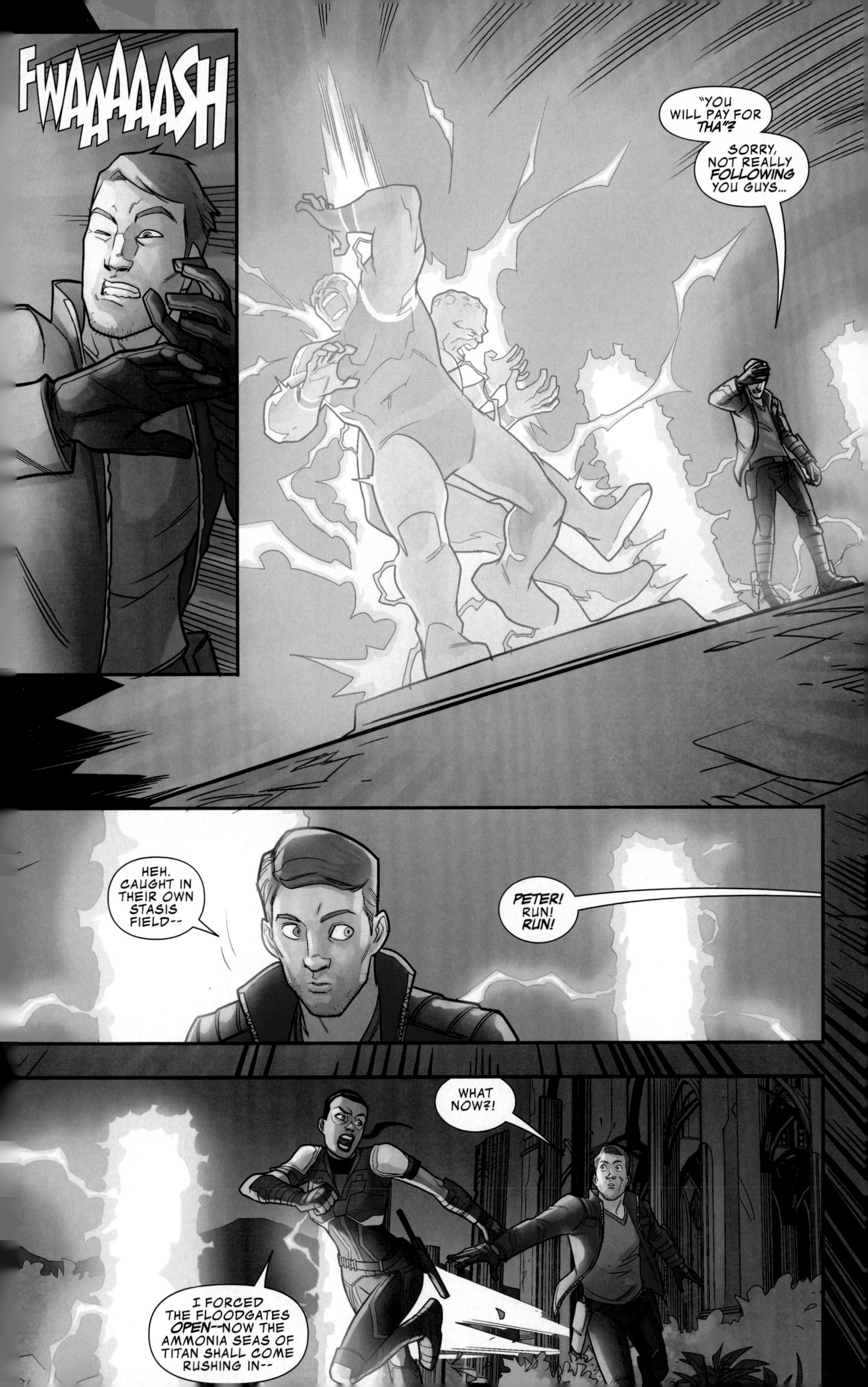
FWAAAAASH
"YOU WILL PAY FOR THA"?
SORRY, NOT REALLY FOLLOWING YOU GUYS...
HEH. CAUGHT IN THEIR OWN STASIS FIELD--
PETER! RUN! RUN!
WHAT NOW?!
I FORCED THE FLOODGATES OPEN--NOW THE AMMONIA SEAS OF TITAN SHALL COME RUSHING IN--

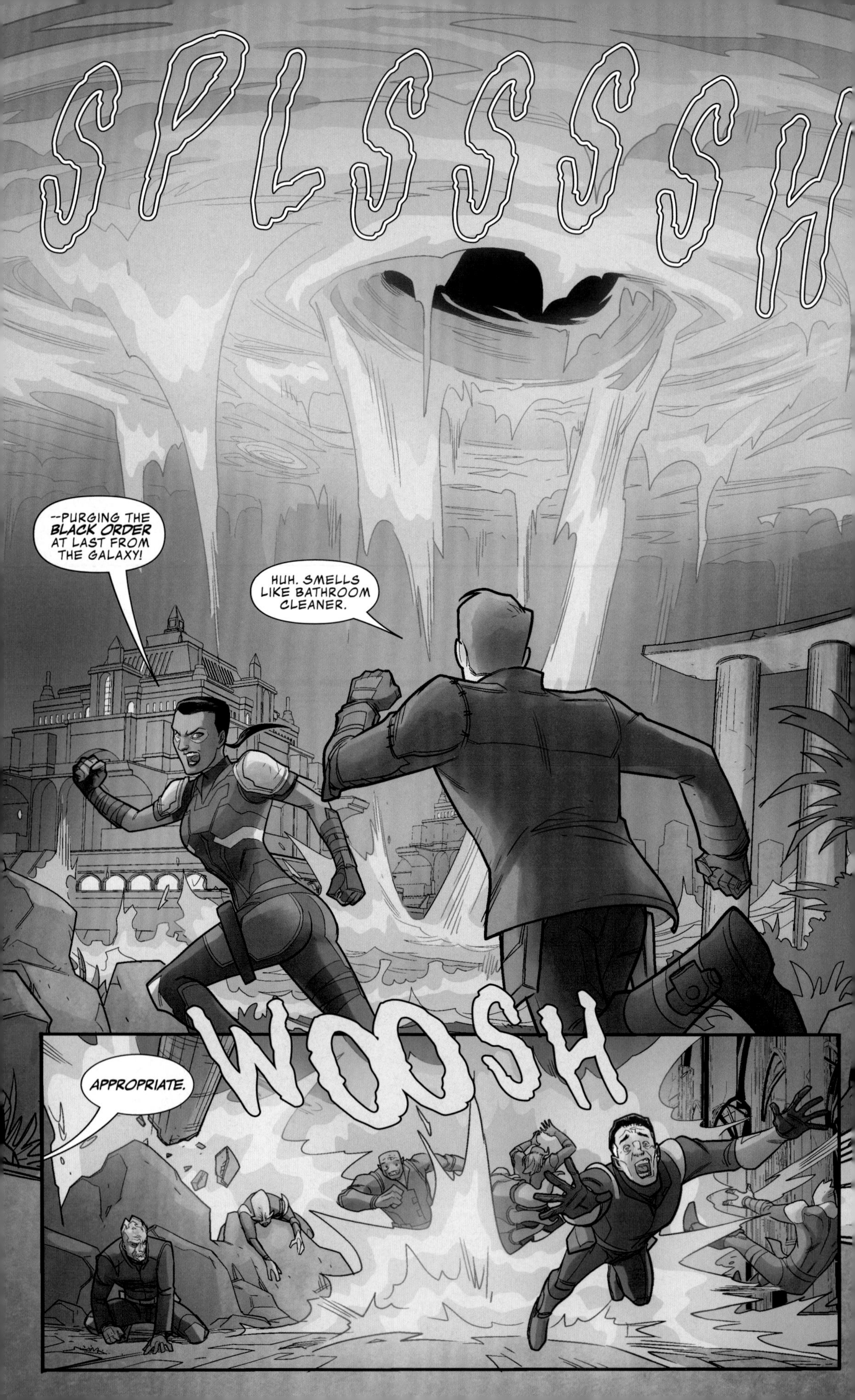
SPLSSSSH
--PURGING THE BLACK ORDER AT LAST FROM THE GALAXY!
HUH. SMELLS LIKE BATHROOM CLEANER.
WOOSH
APPROPRIATE.

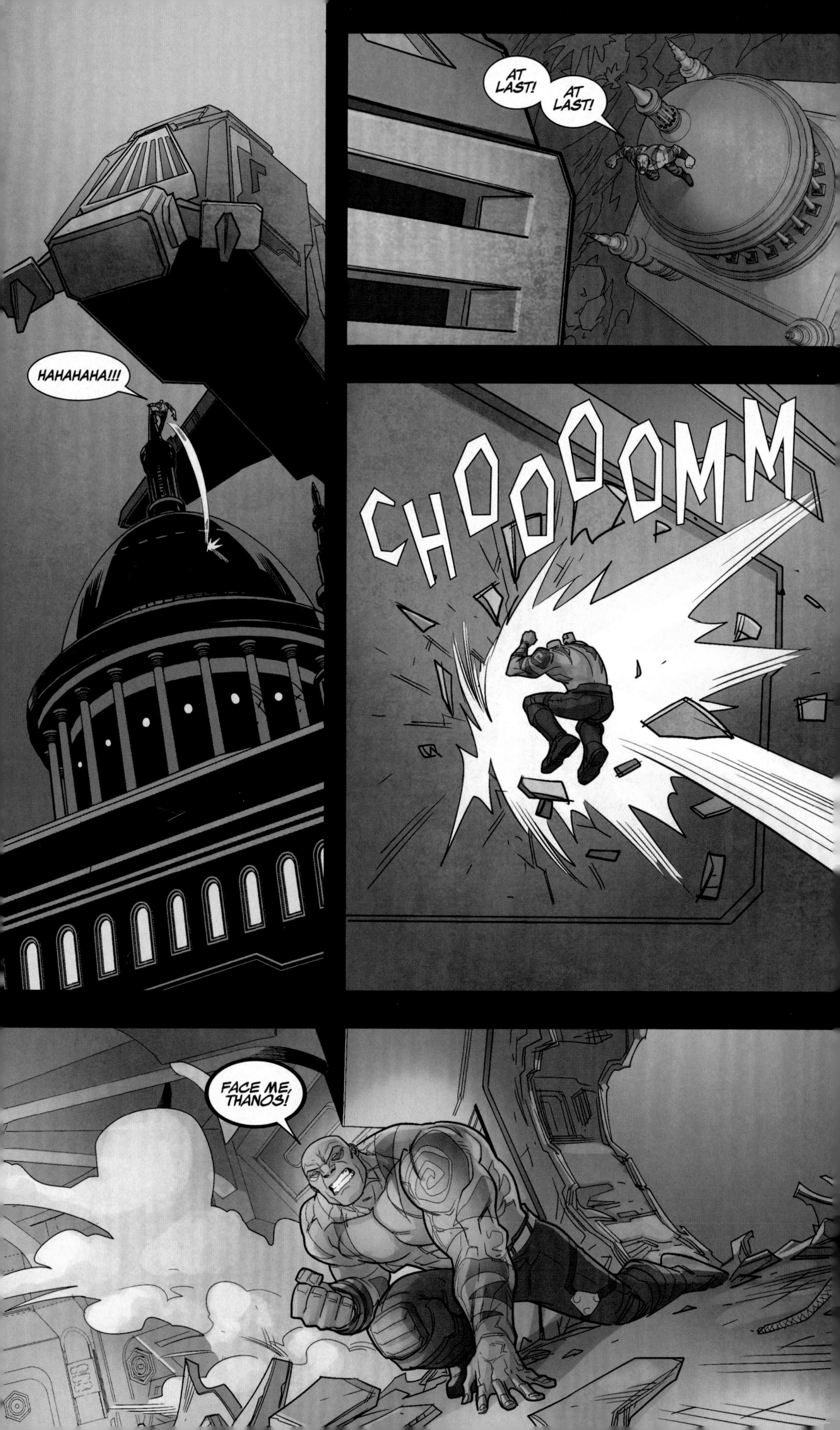
AT LAST!
AT LAST!
HAHAHAHA!!!
CHOOOOMM
FACE ME, THANOS!

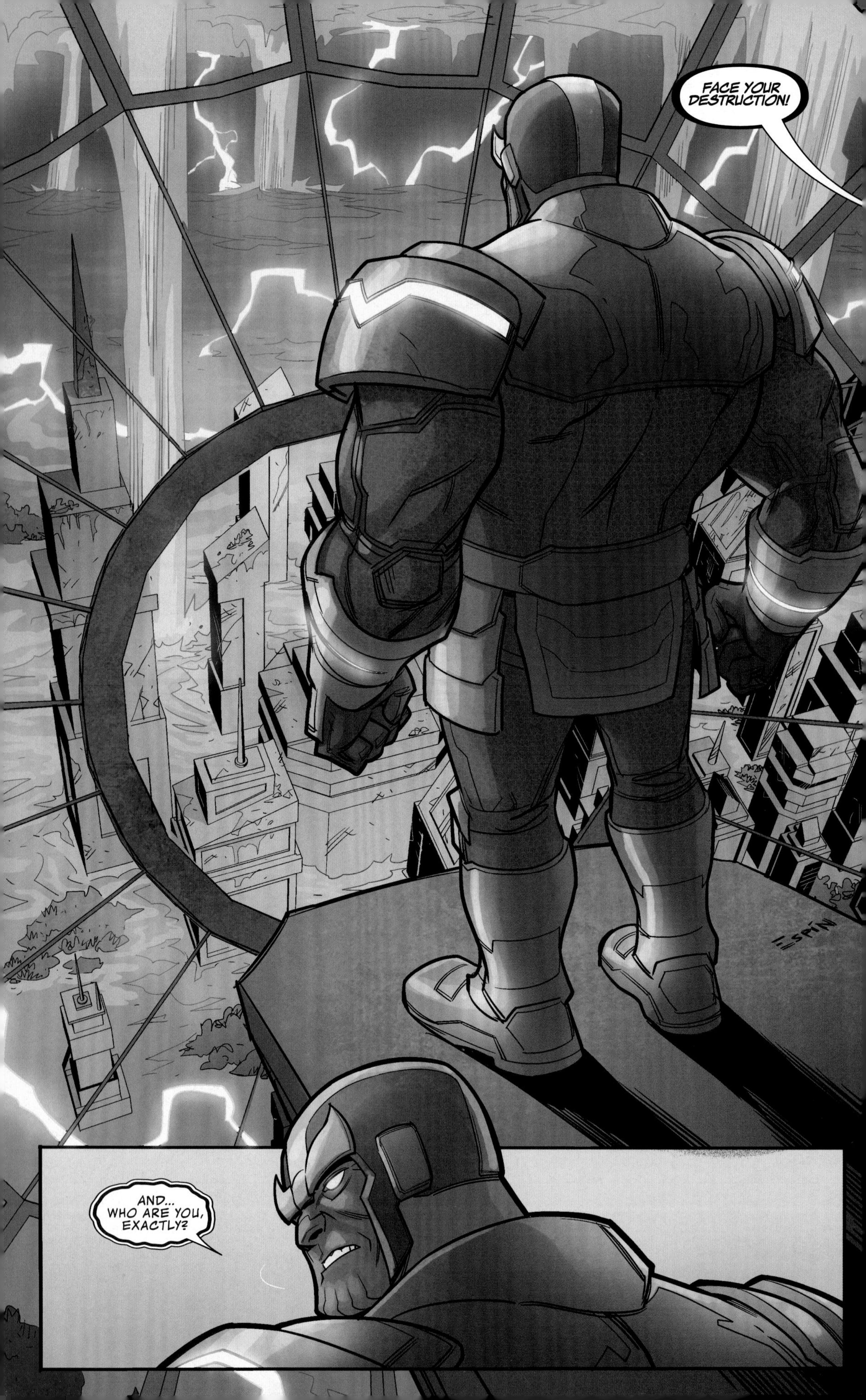
FACE YOUR DESTRUCTION!
ESPIN
AND... WHO ARE YOU, EXACTLY?

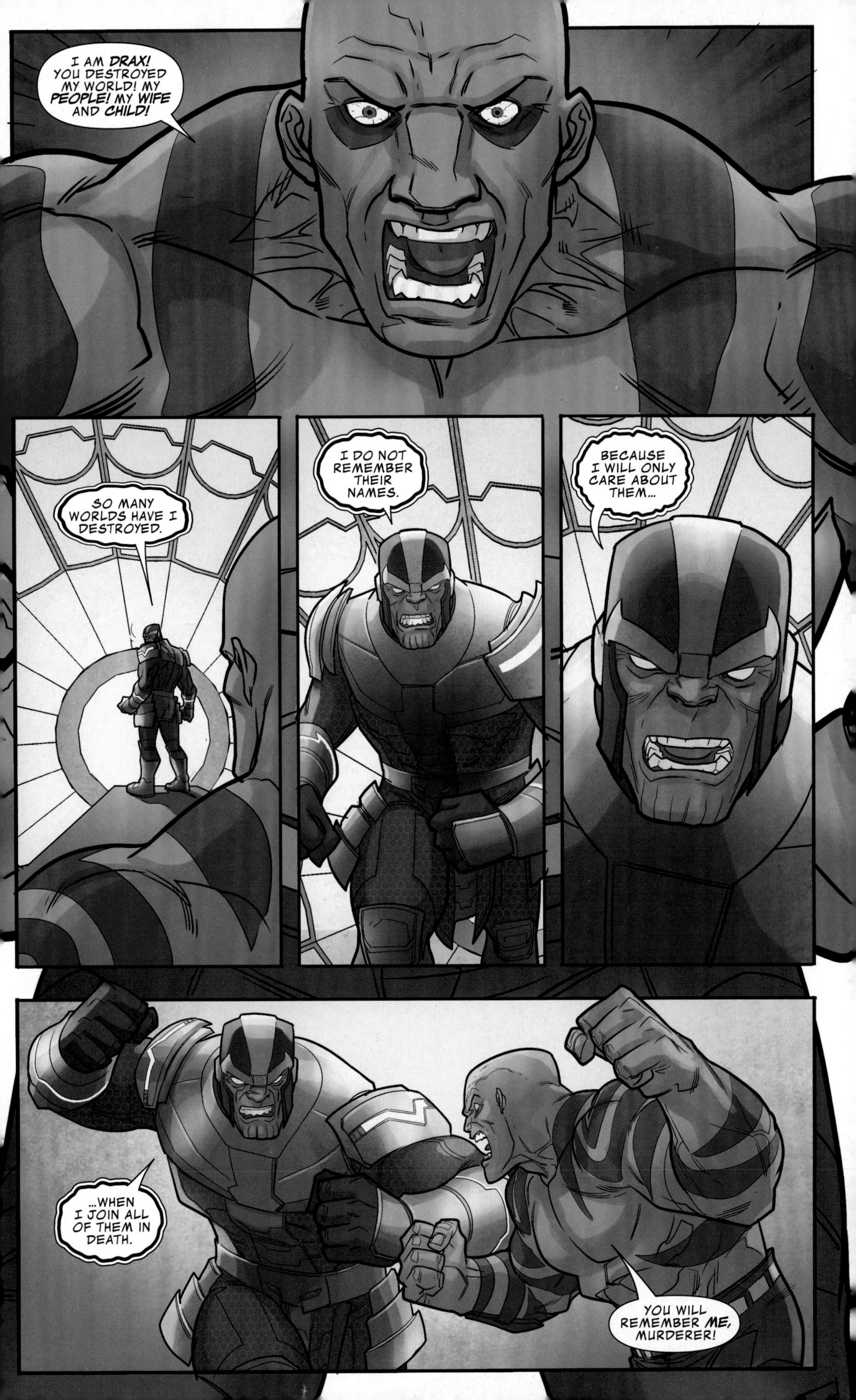
I AM DRAX! YOU DESTROYED MY WORLD! MY PEOPLE! MY WIFE AND CHILD!
SO MANY WORLDS HAVE I DESTROYED.
I DO NOT REMEMBER THEIR NAMES.
BECAUSE I WILL ONLY CARE ABOUT THEM...
...WHEN I JOIN ALL OF THEM IN DEATH.
YOU WILL REMEMBER ME, MURDERER!

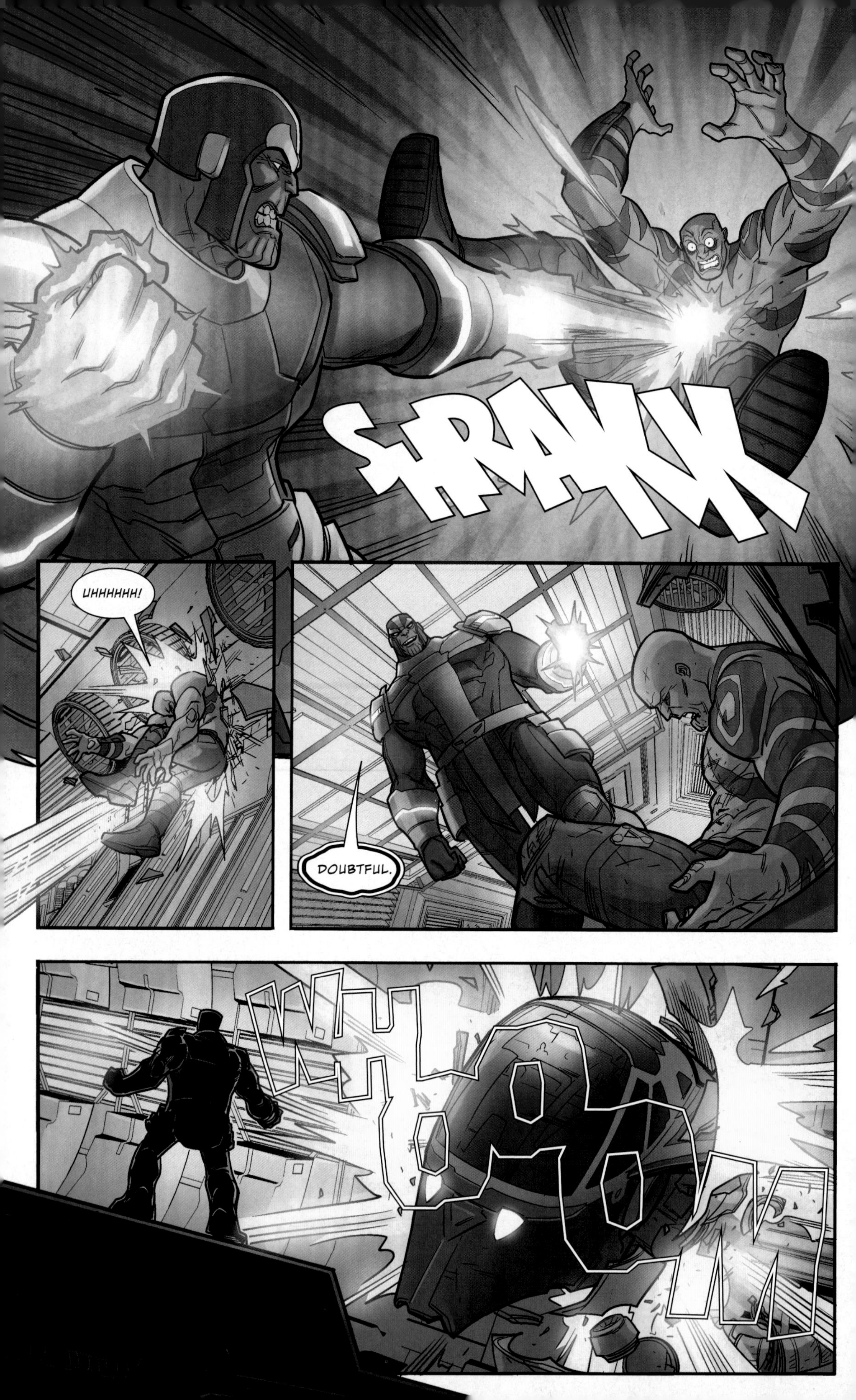
SHRAKK
UHHHHHH!
DOUBTFUL.
WHOOOM

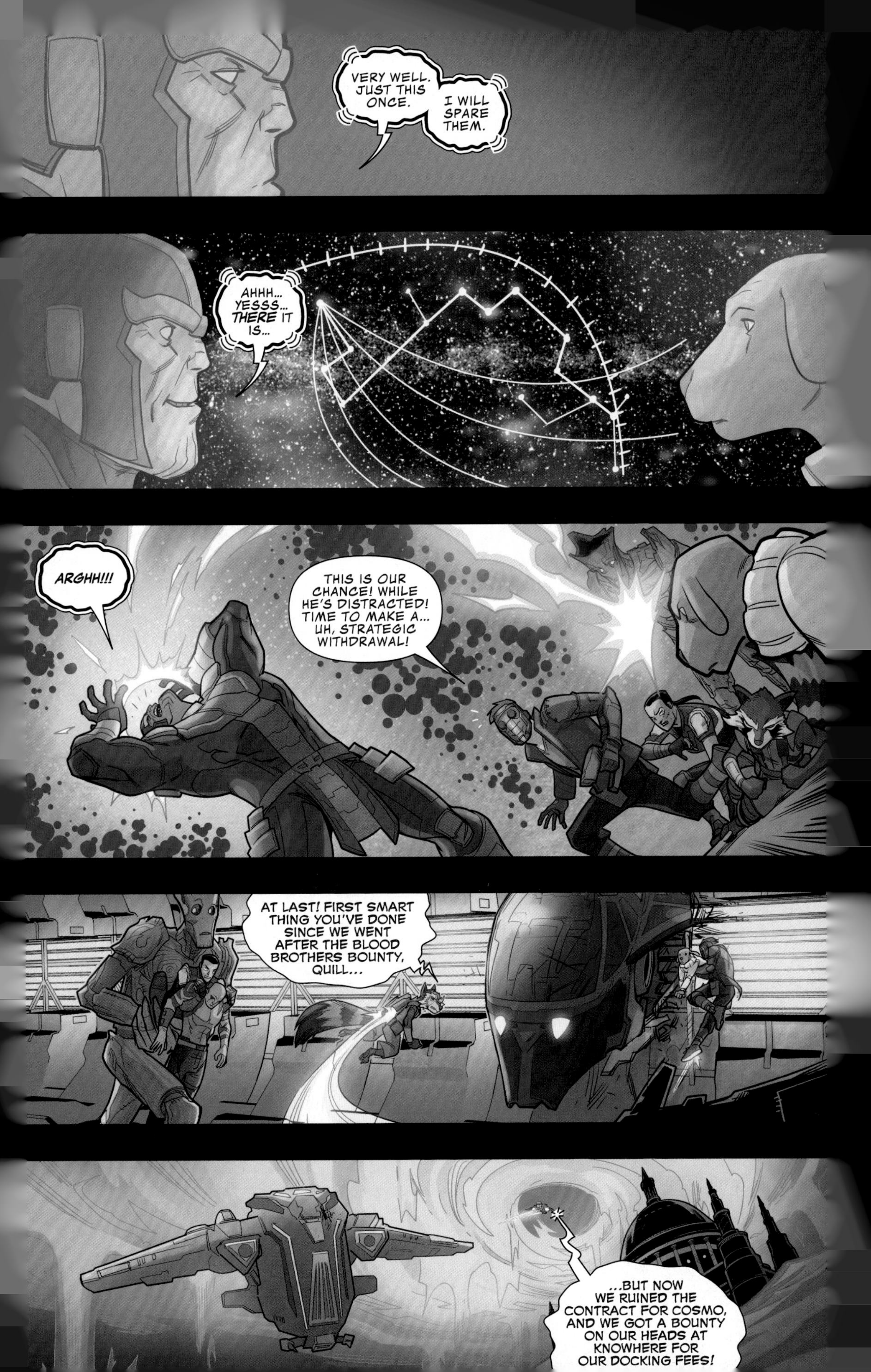

VERY WELL. JUST THIS ONCE.
I WILL SPARE THEM.
AHHH... YESSS... THERE IT IS...
ARGHH!!!
THIS IS OUR CHANCE! WHILE HE'S DISTRACTED! TIME TO MAKE A... UH, STRATEGIC WITHDRAWAL!
AT LAST! FIRST SMART THING YOU'VE DONE SINCE WE WENT AFTER THE BLOOD BROTHERS BOUNTY, QUILL...
...BUT NOW WE RUINED THE CONTRACT FOR COSMO, AND WE GOT A BOUNTY ON OUR HEADS AT KNOWHERE FOR OUR DOCKING FEES!

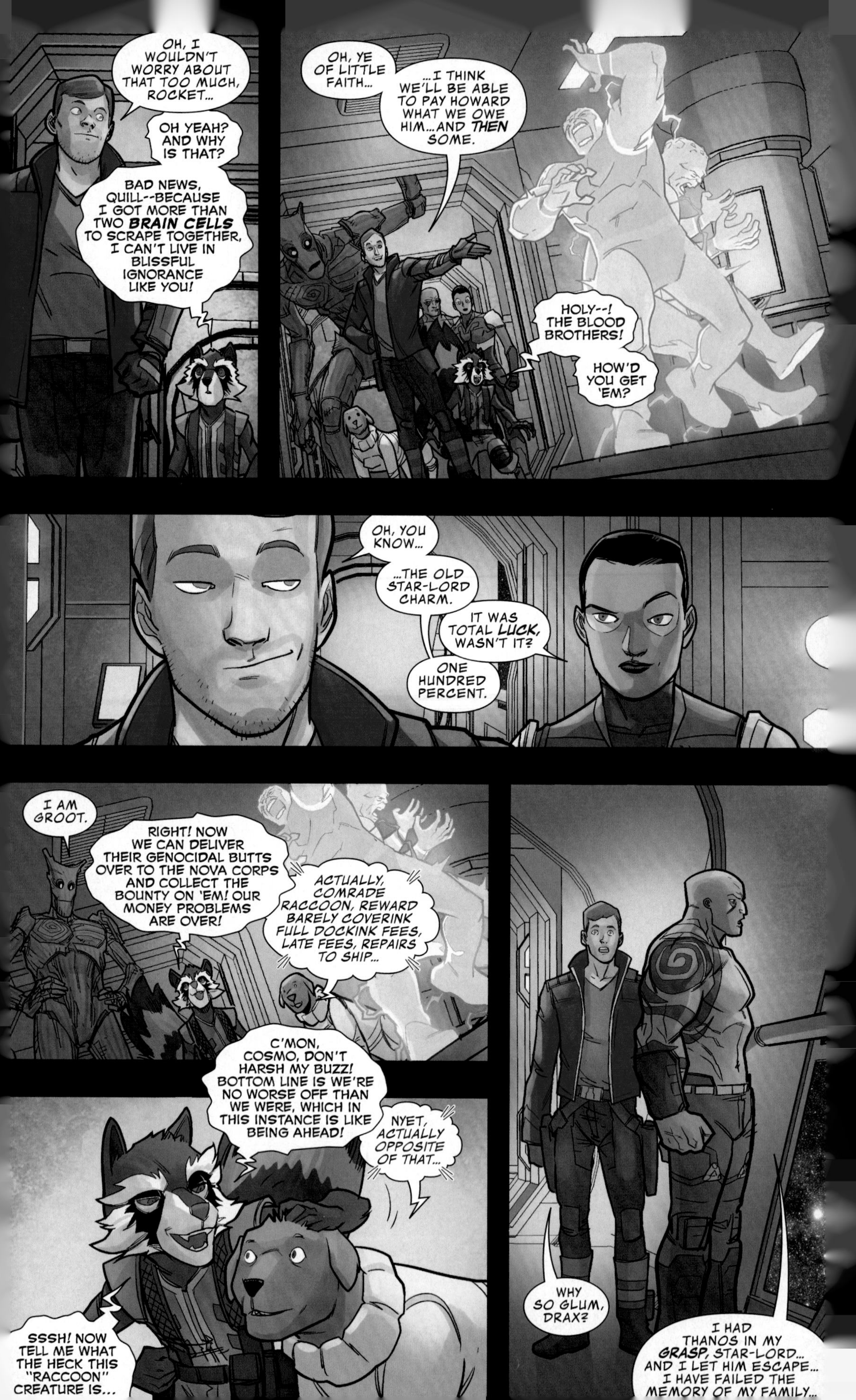
OH, I WOULDN'T WORRY ABOUT THAT TOO MUCH, ROCKET...
OH YEAH? AND WHY IS THAT?
BAD NEWS, QUILL--BECAUSE I GOT MORE THAN TWO BRAIN CELLS TO SCRAPE TOGETHER, I CAN'T LIVE IN BLISSFUL IGNORANCE LIKE YOU!
OH, YE OF LITTLE FAITH...
...I THINK WE'LL BE ABLE TO PAY HOWARD WHAT WE OWE HIM...AND THEN SOME.
HOLY--! THE BLOOD BROTHERS!
HOW'D YOU GET 'EM?
OH, YOU KNOW...
...THE OLD STAR-LORD CHARM.
IT WAS TOTAL LUCK, WASN'T IT?
ONE HUNDRED PERCENT.
I AM GROOT.
RIGHT! NOW WE CAN DELIVER THEIR GENOCIDAL BUTTS OVER TO THE NOVA CORPS AND COLLECT THE BOUNTY ON 'EM! OUR MONEY PROBLEMS ARE OVER!
ACTUALLY, COMRADE RACCOON, REWARD BARELY COVERINK FULL DOCKINK FEES, LATE FEES, REPAIRS TO SHIP...
C'MON, COSMO, DON'T HARSH MY BUZZ! BOTTOM LINE IS WE'RE NO WORSE OFF THAN WE WERE, WHICH IN THIS INSTANCE IS LIKE BEING AHEAD!
NYET, ACTUALLY OPPOSITE OF THAT...
SSSH! NOW TELL ME WHAT THE HECK THIS "RACCOON" CREATURE IS...
WHY SO GLUM, DRAX?
I HAD THANOS IN MY GRASP, STAR-LORD... AND I LET HIM ESCAPE... I HAVE FAILED THE MEMORY OF MY FAMILY...

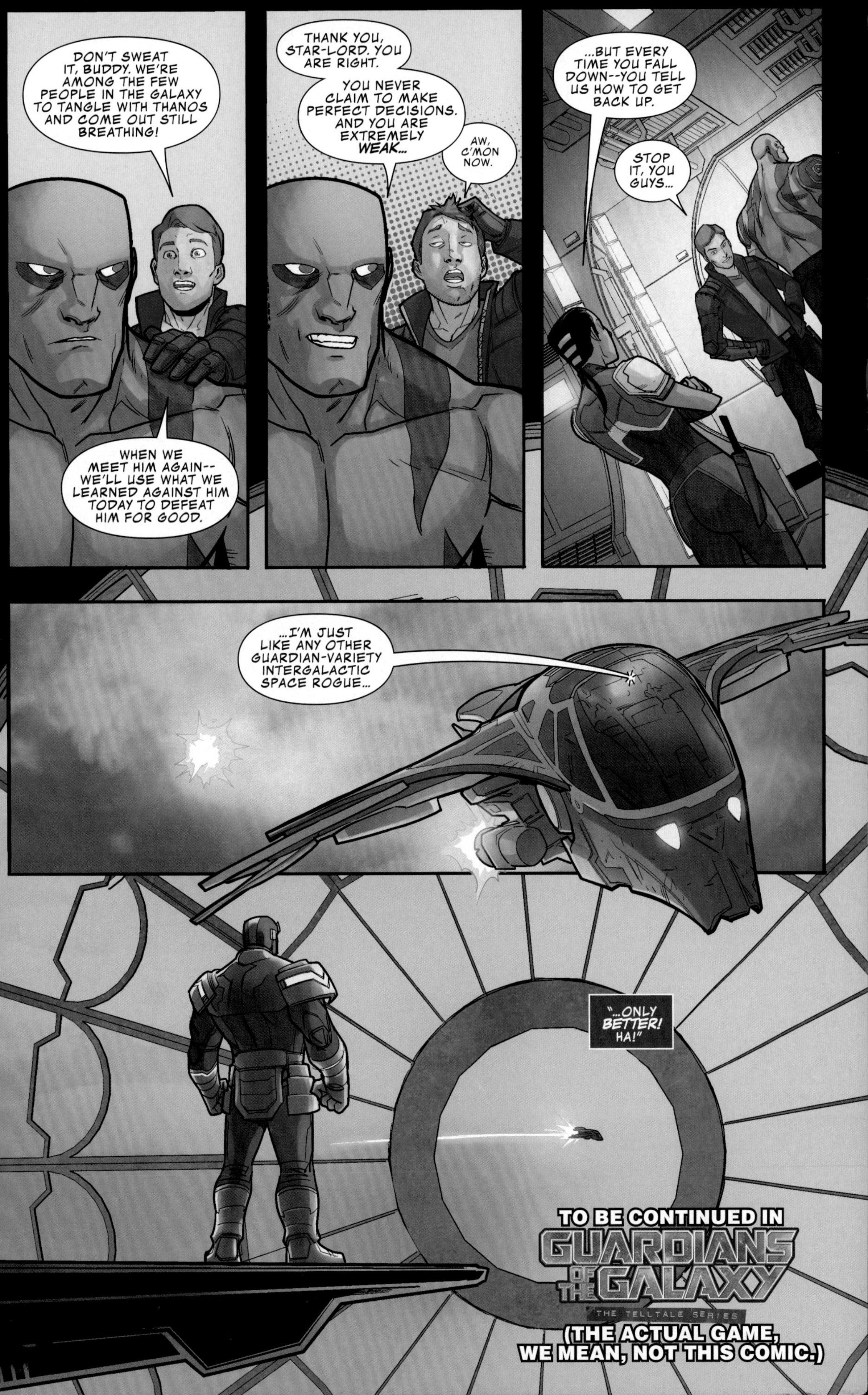
DON'T SWEAT IT, BUDDY. WE'RE AMONG THE FEW PEOPLE IN THE GALAXY TO TANGLE WITH THANOS AND COME OUT STILL BREATHING!
WHEN WE MEET HIM AGAIN-- WE'LL USE WHAT WE LEARNED AGAINST HIM TODAY TO DEFEAT HIM FOR GOOD.
THANK YOU, STAR-LORD. YOU ARE RIGHT.
YOU NEVER CLAIM TO MAKE PERFECT DECISIONS. AND YOU ARE EXTREMELY WEAK...
AW, C'MON NOW.
...BUT EVERY TIME YOU FALL DOWN--YOU TELL US HOW TO GET BACK UP.
STOP IT, YOU GUYS...
...I'M JUST LIKE ANY OTHER GUARDIAN-VARIETY INTERGALACTIC SPACE ROGUE...
"...ONLY BETTER! HA!"
TO BE CONTINUED IN
GUARDIANS OF THE GALAXY
THE TELLTALE SERIES
(THE ACTUAL GAME, WE MEAN, NOT THIS COMIC.)

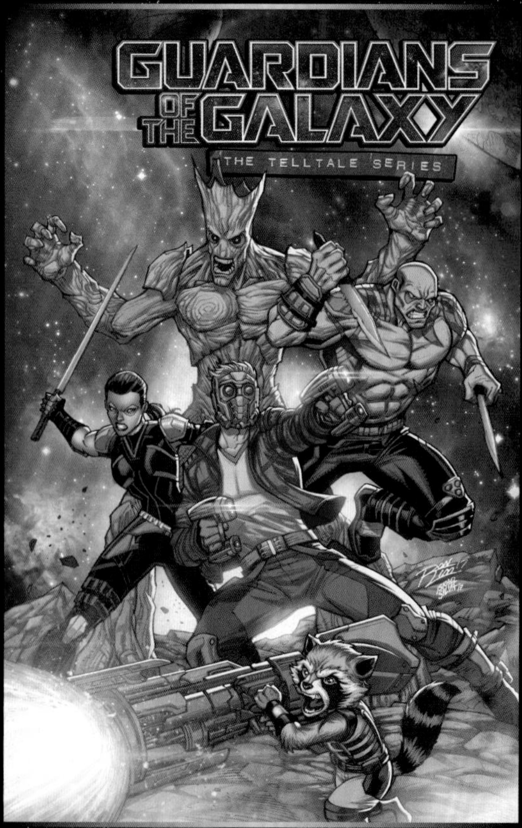
GUARDIANS OF THE GALAXY
THE TELLTALE SERIES

#1 VARIANT BY RON LIM & ISRAEL SILVA

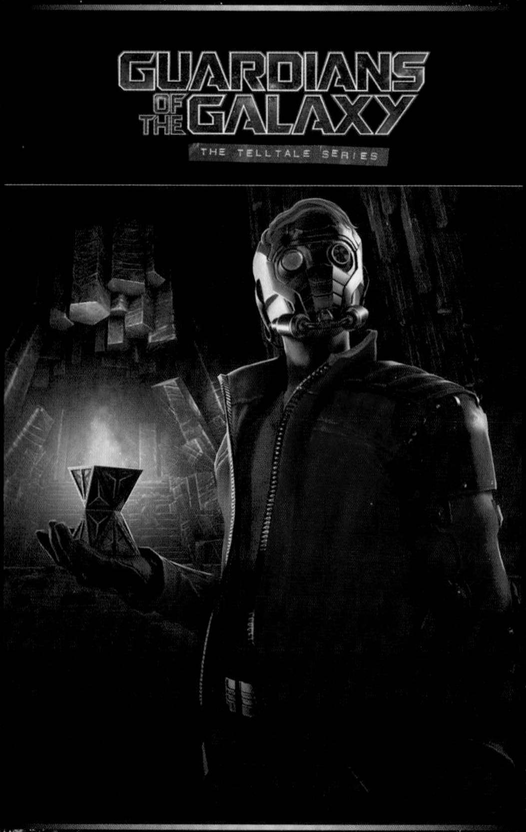
GUARDIANS OF THE GALAXY
THE TELLTALE SERIES

#1 GAME VARIANT

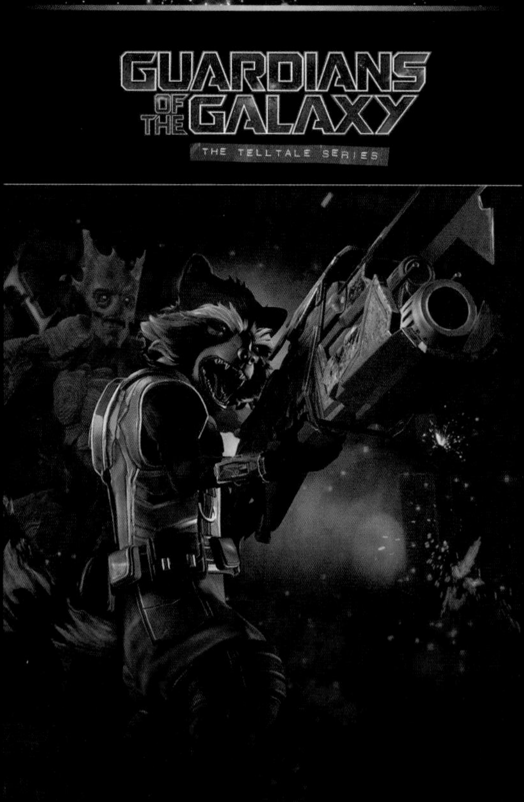
GUARDIANS OF THE GALAXY
THE TELLTALE SERIES

#2 GAME VARIANT

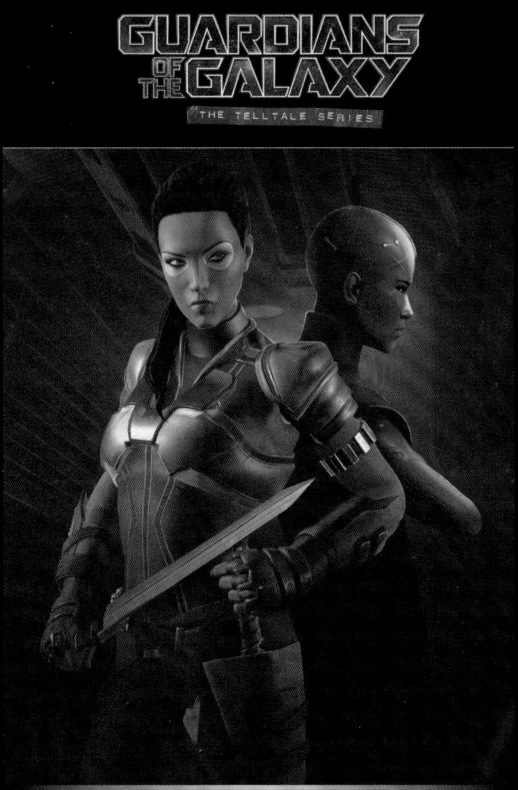
GUARDIANS OF THE GALAXY
THE TELLTALE SERIES

#3 GAME VARIANT

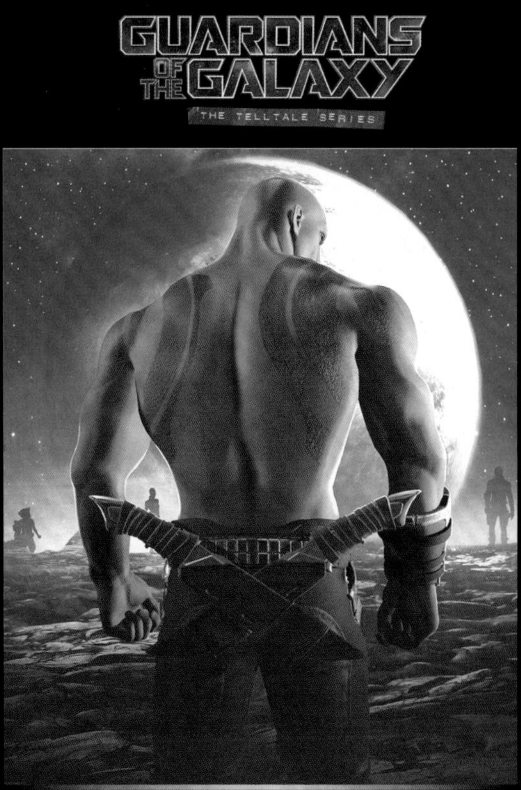
GUARDIANS OF THE GALAXY
THE TELLTALE SERIES

#4 GAME VARIANT

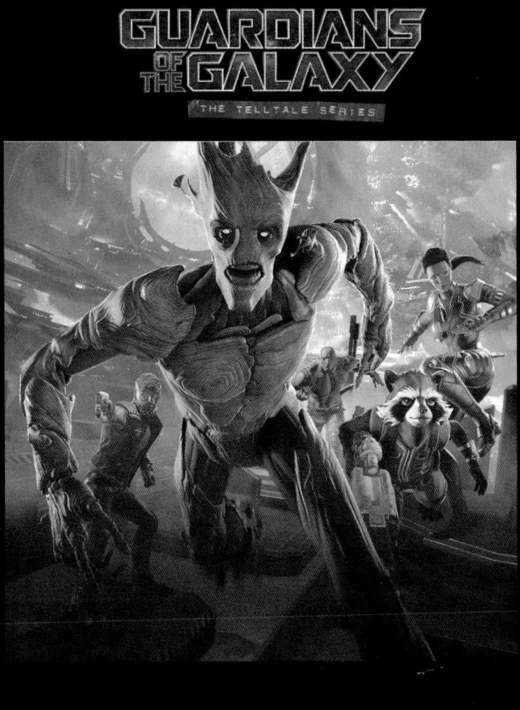
GUARDIANS OF THE GALAXY
THE TELLTALE SERIES

#5 GAME VARIANT

STAR-LORD AND *MILANO* SHIP DESIGNS

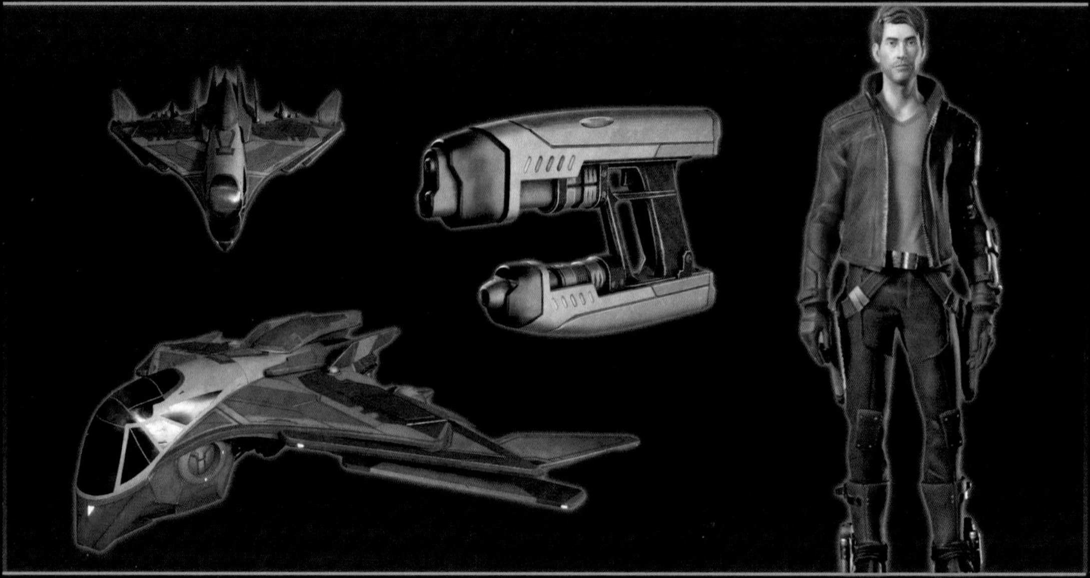

EARLY STAR-LORD CHARACTER CONCEPT BY TELLTALE GAMES

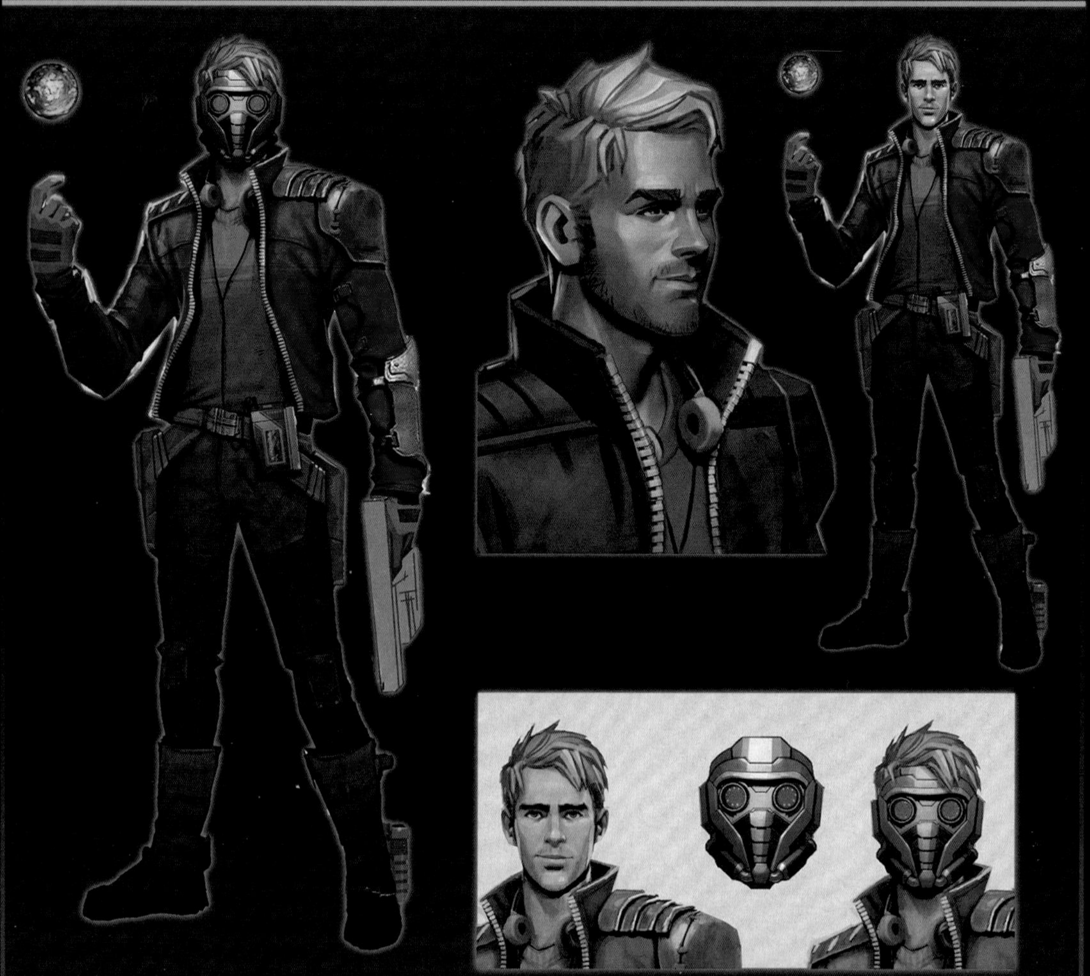

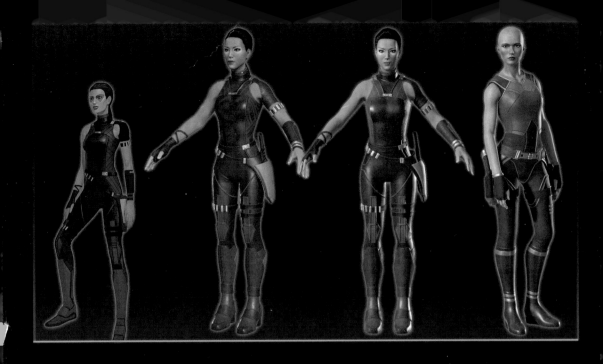

HALA THE ACCUSER DESIGNS

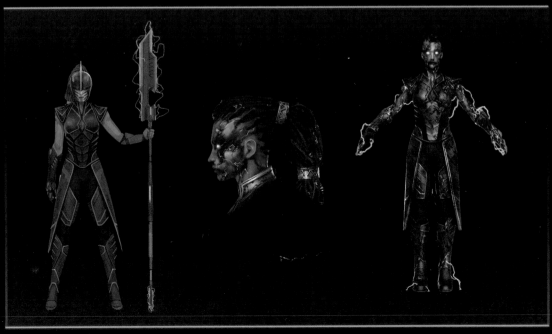

HALA'S DAMAGE STATE DESIGN CAN MANIFEST IN THE GAME — BASED ON YOUR CHOICE.

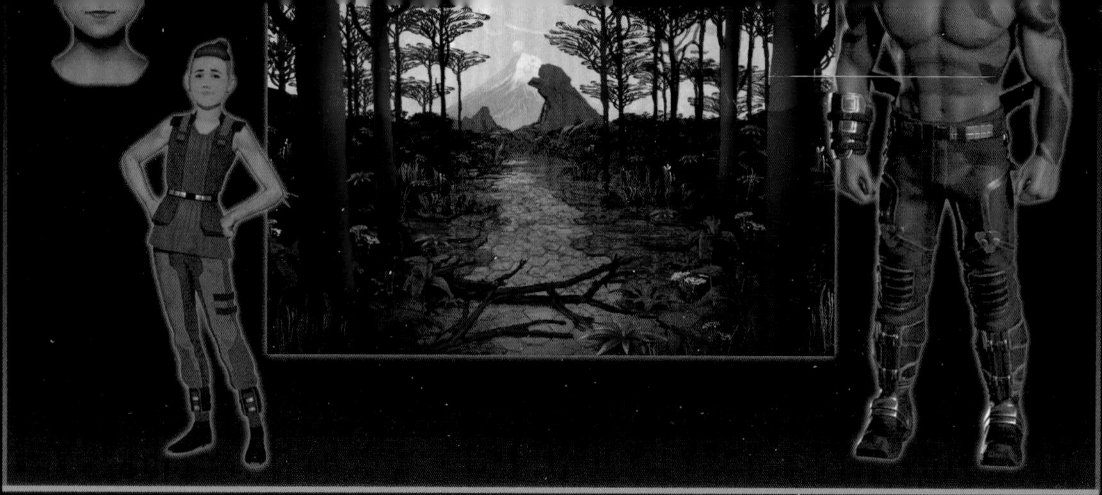

FUNKO POP! – HALA FROM MARVEL'S
GUARDIANS OF THE GALAXY: THE TELLTALE SERIES

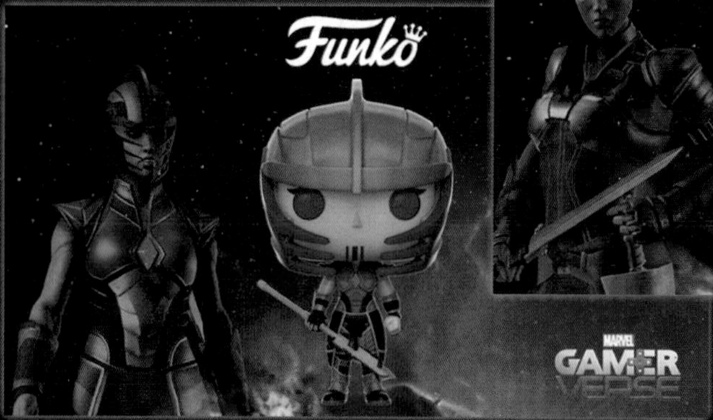
Funko
MARVEL
GAMERVERSE

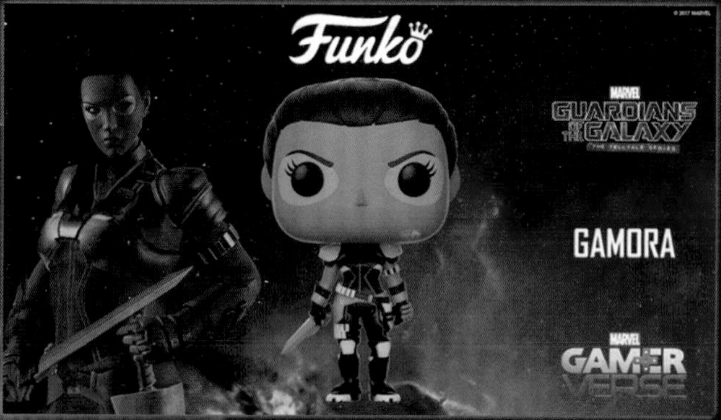
Funko
MARVEL
GUARDIANS OF THE GALAXY
THE TELLTALE SERIES
GAMORA
MARVEL
GAMERVERSE

FUNKO POP! – GAMORA FROM MARVEL'S
GUARDIANS OF THE GALAXY: THE TELLTALE SERIES

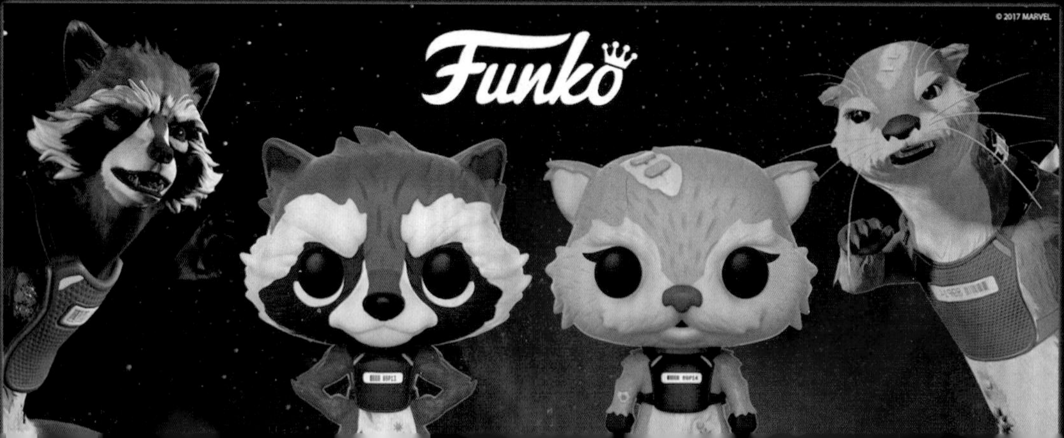
© 2017 MARVEL
Funko